Travel phrasebooks co
«Everything Will Be O

M000223219

PHRASEBOOK
— HEBREW —

THE MOST IMPORTANT PHRASES

This phrasebook contains
the most important
phrases and questions
for basic communication
Everything you need
to survive overseas

T&P BOOKS

By Andrey Taranov

English-Hebrew phrasebook & mini dictionary

By Andrey Taranov

The collection of "Everything Will Be Okay" travel phrasebooks published by T&P Books is designed for people traveling abroad for tourism and business. The phrasebooks contain what matters most - the essentials for basic communication. This is an indispensable set of phrases to "survive" while abroad.

You'll also find a mini dictionary with 250 useful words required for everyday communication - the names of months and days of the week, measurements, family members, and more.

T&P Books Publishing
www.tpbooks.com

ISBN: 978-1-78716-977-7

This book is also available in E-book formats.
Please visit www.tpbooks.com or the major online bookstores.

FOREWORD

The collection of "Everything Will Be Okay" travel phrasebooks published by T&P Books is designed for people traveling abroad for tourism and business. The phrasebooks contain what matters most - the essentials for basic communication. This is an indispensable set of phrases to "survive" while abroad.

This phrasebook will help you in most cases where you need to ask something, get directions, find out how much something costs, etc. It can also resolve difficult communication situations where gestures just won't help.

This book contains a lot of phrases that have been grouped according to the most relevant topics. You'll also find a mini dictionary with useful words - numbers, time, calendar, colors...

Take "Everything Will Be Okay" phrasebook with you on the road and you'll have an irreplaceable traveling companion who will help you find your way out of any situation and teach you to not fear speaking with foreigners.

TABLE OF CONTENTS

T&P Books Publishing

PRONUNCIATION

Letter's name	Letter	Hebrew example	T&P phonetic alphabet	English example
Alef	א	אריה	[a], [ɑ:]	bath, to pass
	א	אחד	[ɛ], [ɛ:]	habit, bad
	א	מָאָה	['] (hamza)	glottal stop
Bet	ב	בית	[b]	baby, book
Gimel	ג	גמל	[g]	game, gold
Gimel+geresh	ג׳	ג׳ונגל	[ʤ]	joke, general
Dalet	ד	דג	[d]	day, doctor
Hei	ה	הר	[h]	home, have
Vav	ו	וסת	[v]	very, river
Zayin	ז	זאב	[z]	zebra, please
Zayin+geresh	ז׳	ז׳ורנָל	[ʒ]	forge, pleasure
Chet	ח	חוט	[x]	as in Scots 'loch'
Tet	ט	טוב	[t]	tourist, trip
Yud	י	יום	[j]	yes, New York
Kaph	ך כ	בריש	[k]	clock, kiss
Lamed	ל	לחם	[l]	lace, people
Mem	ם מ	מלך	[m]	magic, milk
Nun	ן נ	נר	[n]	name, normal
Samech	ס	סוס	[s]	city, boss
Ayin	ע	עין	[a], [ɑ:]	bath, to pass
	ע	תשעים	['] (ayn)	voiced pharyngeal fricative
Pei	ף פ	פיל	[p]	pencil, private
Tsadi	צ ץ	צעצוע	[ʦ]	cats, tsetse fly
Tsadi+geresh	צ׳ ץ׳	צ׳ק	[ʧ]	church, French
Qoph	ק	קוף	[k]	clock, kiss
Resh	ר	רכבת	[r]	French (guttural) R
Shin	ש	שלחן, עָשׂרים	[s], [ʃ]	city, machine
Tav	ת	תפוז	[t]	tourist, trip

LIST OF ABBREVIATIONS

Explication

⇨ man	-	addressing a man
⇨ woman	-	addressing a woman
couple, men ⇨	-	a couple or men are speaking
man ⇨	-	man is speaking
man ⇨ man	-	a man speaks to a man
man ⇨ woman	-	a man speaks to a woman
woman ⇨	-	woman is speaking
woman ⇨ man	-	a woman speaks to a man
woman ⇨ woman	-	a woman speaks to a woman
women ⇨	-	women are speaking

English abbreviations

ab.	-	about
adj	-	adjective
adv	-	adverb
anim.	-	animate
as adj	-	attributive noun used as adjective
e.g.	-	for example
etc.	-	et cetera
fam.	-	familiar
fem.	-	feminine
form.	-	formal
inanim.	-	inanimate
masc.	-	masculine
math	-	mathematics
mil.	-	military
n	-	noun
pl	-	plural
pron.	-	pronoun
sb	-	somebody
sing.	-	singular
sth	-	something
v aux	-	auxiliary verb

vi	-	intransitive verb
vi, vt	-	intransitive, transitive verb
vt	-	transitive verb

Hebrew abbreviations

ז	-	masculine
ז"ר	-	masculine plural
ז , נ	-	masculine, feminine
נ	-	feminine
נ"ר	-	feminine plural

HEBREW PHRASEBOOK

This section contains important phrases that may come in handy in various real-life situations.
The phrasebook will help you ask for directions, clarify a price, buy tickets, and order food at a restaurant

T&P Books Publishing

PHRASEBOOK
CONTENTS

T&P Books Publishing

Excuse me, ... (☞ man)	slaχ li, ... **סלח לי, ...**
Excuse me, ... (☞ woman)	silχi li, ... **סלחי לי, ...**
Hello.	ʃalom. **שלום.**
Thank you.	toda. **תודה.**
Good bye.	lehitra'ot. **להתראות.**

Yes.	ken. **כן.**
No.	lo. **לא.**
I don't know. (man ☞)	ani lo yo'de'a. **אני לא יודע.**
I don't know. (woman ☞)	ani lo yo'da'at. **אני לא יודעת.**
Where?	Where to?	When?	eifo?	le'an?	matai? **איפה?	לאן?	מתי?**

I need ... (man ☞)	ani tsariχ ... **אני צריך ...**
I need ... (woman ☞)	ani tsriχa ... **אני צריכה ...**
I want ... (man ☞)	ani rotse ... **אני רוצה ...**
I want ... (woman ☞)	ani rotsa ... **אני רוצה ...**

Do you have ...? (☞ man)	ha'im yeʃ leχa ...? **האם יש לך ...?**
Do you have ...? (☞ woman)	ha'im yeʃ laχ ...? **האם יש לך ...?**
Is there a ... here?	ha'im yeʃ po ...? **האם יש פה ...?**

May I ...? (man ☞)	ha'im ani yaχol ...? **האם אני יכול ...?**
May I ...? (woman ☞)	ha'im ani yeχola ...? **האם אני יכולה ...?**
..., please (polite request)	..., bevakaʃa **..., בבקשה**

I'm looking for ... (man ☞)	ani meχapes ... אני מחפש ...
I'm looking for ... (woman ☞)	ani meχa'peset ... אני מחפשת ...
the restroom	ʃerutim שירותים
an ATM	kaspomat כספומט
a pharmacy (drugstore)	beit mer'kaχat בית מרקחת
a hospital	beit χolim בית חולים
the police station	taχanat miʃtara תחנת משטרה
the subway	ra'kevet taχtit רכבת תחתית
a taxi	monit, 'teksi מונית, טקסי
the train station	taχanat ra'kevet תחנת רכבת

My name is ...	kor'im li ... קוראים לי ...
What's your name? (☞ man)	eiχ kor'im leχa? איך קוראים לך?
What's your name? (☞ woman)	eiχ kor'im laχ? איך קוראים לך?
Could you please help me? (☞ man)	ha'im ata yaχol la'azor li? האם אתה יכול לעזור לי?
Could you please help me? (☞ woman)	ha'im at yeχola la'azor li? האם את יכולה לעזור לי?
I've got a problem.	yeʃ li be'aya. יש לי בעייה.
I don't feel well. (man ☞)	ani lo margiʃ tov. אני לא מרגיש טוב.
I don't feel well. (woman ☞)	ani lo margiʃa tov. אני לא מרגישה טוב.
Call an ambulance! (☞ man)	hazmen 'ambulans! הזמן אמבולנס!
Call an ambulance! (☞ woman)	haz'mini 'ambulans! הזמיני אמבולנס!
May I make a call? (man ☞)	ha'im ani yaχol lehitkaʃer? האם אני יכול להתקשר?
May I make a call? (woman ☞)	ha'im ani yeχola lehitkaʃer? האם אני יכולה להתקשר?

I'm sorry. (man ☞)	ani mitsta'er. אני מצטער.
I'm sorry. (woman ☞)	ani mitsta"eret. אני מצטערת.
You're welcome.	ein be'ad ma, bevakaʃa. אין בעד מה, בבקשה.

I, me	ani
	אני
you (inform.) (masc.)	ata
	אתה
you (inform.) (fem.)	at
	את
he	hu
	הוא
she	hi
	היא
they (masc.)	hem
	הם
they (fem.)	hen
	הן
we	a'naχnu
	אנחנו
you (pl) (masc.)	atem
	אתם
you (pl) (fem.)	aten
	אתן
you (sg, form.) (masc.)	ata
	אתה
you (sg, form.) (fem.)	at
	את

ENTRANCE	knisa
	כניסה
EXIT	yetsi'a
	יציאה
OUT OF ORDER	lo po'el
	לא פועל
CLOSED	sagur
	סגור
OPEN	pa'tuaχ
	פתוח
FOR WOMEN	lenaʃim
	לנשים
FOR MEN	ligvarim
	לגברים

Questions

Where?	eifo? איפה?
Where to?	le'an? לאן?
Where from?	me"eifo? מאיפה?
Why?	lama? למה?
For what reason?	me"eizo siba? מאיזו סיבה?
When?	matai? מתי?

How long?	kama zman? כמה זמן?
At what time?	be"eizo ʃa'a? באיזו שעה?
How much?	kama? כמה?
Do you have ...? (⌐ man)	ha'im jeʃ leχa ...? האם יש לך ...?
Do you have ...? (⌐ woman)	ha'im jeʃ laχ ...? האם יש לך ...?
Where is ...?	eifo ...? איפה ...?

What time is it?	ma haʃa'a? מה השעה?
May I make a call? (man ⌐)	ha'im ani jaχol lehitkaʃer? האם אני יכול להתקשר?
May I make a call? (woman ⌐)	ha'im ani jeχola lehitkaʃer? האם אני יכולה להתקשר?
Who's there?	mi ʃam? מי שם?
Can I smoke here?	ha'im mutar le'aʃen kan? האם מותר לעשן כאן?
May I ...? (man ⌐)	ha'im ani jaχol ...? האם אני יכול ...?
May I ...? (woman ⌐)	ha'im ani jeχola ...? האם אני יכולה ...?

Needs

I'd like … (man ☞)	ha'yiti rotse … הייתי רוצה ...
I'd like … (woman ☞)	ha'yiti rotsa … הייתי רוצה ...
I don't want … (man ☞)	ani lo rotse … אני לא רוצה ...
I don't want … (woman ☞)	ani lo rotsa … אני לא רוצה ...
I'm thirsty. (man ☞)	ani tsame. אני צמא.
I'm thirsty. (woman ☞)	ani tsme'a. אני צמאה.
I want to sleep.	ani rotse liʃon. אני רוצה לישון.
I want … (man ☞)	ani rotse … אני רוצה ...
I want … (woman ☞)	ani rotsa … אני רוצה ...

to wash up	liʃtof panim veya'dayim לשטוף פנים וידיים
to brush my teeth	letsaχ'tseaχ ʃi'nayim לצחצח שיניים
to rest a while	la'nuaχ ktsat לנוח קצת
to change my clothes	lehaχlif bgadim להחליף בגדים
to go back to the hotel	laχazor lamalon לחזור למלון
to buy …	liknot … לקנות ...
to go to …	la'leχet le… ללכת ל ...
to visit …	levaker be… לבקר ב ...
to meet with …	lehipageʃ im… להיפגש עם...
to make a call	letalfen, lehitkaʃer לטלפן, להתקשר

I'm tired. (man ☞)	ani ayef. אני עייף.
I'm tired. (woman ☞)	ani ayefa. אני עייפה.

We are tired. (couple , men ☺)	a'naxnu ayefim. אנחנו עייפים.
We are tired. (women ☺)	anaxnu ayefot. אנחנו עייפות.
I'm cold.	kar li. קר לי.
I'm hot.	xam li. חם לי.
I'm OK.	ani be'seder. אני בסדר.

I need to make a call. (man ☺)	ani tsarix lehitkaʃer. אני צריך להתקשר.
I need to make a call. (woman ☺)	ani tsrixa lehitkaʃer. אני צריכה להתקשר.
I need to go to the restroom. (man ☺)	ani tsarix leʃerutim. אני צריך ללכת לשירותים.
I need to go to the restroom. (woman ☺)	ani tsrixa leʃerutim. אני צריכה ללכת לשירותים.
I have to go. (man ☺)	ani tsarix la'lexet. אני צריך ללכת.
I have to go. (woman ☺)	ani tsrixa la'lexet. אני צריכה ללכת.
I have to go now. (man ☺)	ani xayav la'lexet axʃav. אני חייב ללכת עכשיו.
I have to go now. (woman ☺)	ani xa'yevet la'lexet axʃav. אני חייבת ללכת עכשיו.

Asking for directions

Excuse me, … (man ☞)	slaχ li, ….
	... ,סלח לי
Excuse me, … (woman ☞)	silχi li, ….
	... ,סלחי לי
Where is …?	eifo …?
	?... איפה
Which way is …?	eiχ megi'im le …?
	?... איך מגיעים ל
Could you help me, please? (☞ man)	ha'im ata yaχol la'azor li, bevakaʃa?
	?האם אתה יכול לעזור לי, בבקשה
Could you help me, please? (☞ woman)	ha'im at yeχola la'azor li, bevakaʃa?
	?האם את יכולה לעזור לי, בבקשה

I'm looking for … (man ☞)	ani meχapes …
	... אני מחפש
I'm looking for … (woman ☞)	ani meχa'peset …
	... אני מחפשת
I'm looking for the exit. (man ☞)	ani meχapes et hayetsi'a.
	.אני מחפש את היציאה
I'm looking for the exit. (woman ☞)	ani meχa'peset et hayetsi'a.
	.אני מחפשת את היציאה
I'm going to … (man ☞)	ani holeχ le …
	... אני הולך ל
I'm going to … (woman ☞)	ani ho'leχet le …
	... אני הולכת ל
Am I going the right way to …?	ha'im ani bakivun hanaχon le …?
	?... האם אני בכיוון הנכון ל

Is it far?	ha'im ze raχok?
	?האם זה רחוק
Can I get there on foot?	ha'im efʃar leha'gi'a leʃam ba'regel?
	?האם אפשר להגיע לשם ברגל
Can you show me on the map? (☞ man)	ha'im ata yaχol lehar'ot li al hamapa?
	?האם אתה יכול להראות לי על המפה
Can you show me on the map? (☞ woman)	ha'im at yeχola lehar'ot li al hamapa?
	?האם את יכולה להראות לי על המפה
Show me where we are right now. (☞ man)	har'e li heiχan 'anu nimtsa'im aχʃav.
	.הראה לי היכן אנו נמצאים עכשיו
Show me where we are right now. (☞ woman)	har'i li heiχan 'anu nimtsa'im aχʃav.
	.הראי לי היכן אנו נמצאים עכשיו
Here	kan, po
	כאן, פה
There	ʃam
	שם

This way
lekan
לכאן

Turn right. (⇦ man)
pne ya'mina.
פנה ימינה.

Turn right. (⇦ woman)
pni ya'mina.
פני ימינה.

Turn left. (⇦ man)
pne 'smola.
פנה שמאלה.

Turn left. (⇦ woman)
pni 'smola.
פני שמאלה.

first (second, third) turn
pniya riʃona (ʃniya, ʃliʃit)
פנייה ראשונה (שנייה, שלישית)

to the right
ya'mina
ימינה

to the left
smola
שמאלה

Go straight ahead. (⇦ man)
leχ yaʃar.
לך ישר.

Go straight ahead. (⇦ woman)
leχi yaʃar.
לכי ישר.

Signs

WELCOME!	bruχim haba'im! **ברוכים הבאים!**
ENTRANCE	knisa **כניסה**
EXIT	yetsi'a **יציאה**
PUSH	dχof **דחוף**
PULL	mʃoχ **משוך**
OPEN	pa'tuaχ **פתוח**
CLOSED	sagur **סגור**
FOR WOMEN	lenaʃim **לנשים**
FOR MEN	ligvarim **לגברים**
GENTLEMEN, GENTS	gvarim **גברים**
WOMEN	naʃim **נשים**
DISCOUNTS	hanaχot **הנחות**
SALE	mivtsa **מבצע**
FREE	χinam, beχinam **חינם, בחינם**
NEW!	χadaʃ! **חדש!**
ATTENTION!	sim lev! **שים לב!**
NO VACANCIES	ein mekomot pnuyim **אין מקומות פנויים**
RESERVED	ʃamur **שמור**
ADMINISTRATION	hanhala **הנהלה**
STAFF ONLY	le'ovdim bilvad **לעובדים בלבד**

BEWARE OF THE DOG!	zehirut, 'kelev! זהירות כלב!
NO SMOKING!	asur le'aʃen! אסור לעשן!
DO NOT TOUCH!	asur la'ga'at! אסור לגעת!
DANGEROUS	mesukan מסוכן
DANGER	sakana סכנה
HIGH VOLTAGE	metaχ ga'voha מתח גבוה
NO SWIMMING!	asur lisχot! אסור לשחות!

OUT OF ORDER	lo po'el לא פועל
FLAMMABLE	dalik דליק
FORBIDDEN	asur אסור
NO TRESPASSING!	ein ma'avar אין מעבר
WET PAINT	tseva laχ, 'tseva tari צבע לח, צבע טרי

CLOSED FOR RENOVATIONS	sagur leʃiputsim סגור לשיפוצים
WORKS AHEAD	avodot bakviʃ עבודות בכביש
DETOUR	ma'akaf מעקף

Transportation. General phrases

plane	matos
	מטוס
train	ra'kevet
	רכבת
bus	'otobus
	אוטובוס
ferry	ma'a'boret
	מעבורת
taxi	monit
	מונית
car	meχonit
	מכונית

schedule	luaχ zmanim
	לוח זמנים
Where can I see the schedule?	heiχan efʃar lir'ot et 'luaχ hazmanim?
	היכן אפשר לראות את לוח הזמנים?
workdays (weekdays)	yemei avoda
	ימי עבודה
weekends	sofei ʃa'vu'a
	סופי שבוע
holidays	χagim
	חגים

DEPARTURE	hamra'a
	המראה
ARRIVAL	neχita
	נחיתה
DELAYED	ikuv
	עיכוב
CANCELLED	bitul
	ביטול

next (train, etc.)	haba /haba'a/
	הבא /הבאה/
first	riʃon /riʃona/
	ראשון /ראשונה/
last	aχaron /aχrona/
	אחרון /אחרונה/

When is the next ...?	matai ha... haba /haba'a/?
	מתי ה ... הבא /הבאה/?
When is the first ...?	matai ha... hariʃon /hariʃona/?
	מתי ה ... הראשון /הראשונה/?

When is the last …?	matai ha… ha'aχaron /ha'aχrona/? מתי ה ... האחרון /האחרונה/?
transfer (change of trains, etc.)	haχlafa, ko'nekʃen החלפה, קונקשן
to make a transfer	la'asot haχlafa לעשות החלפה
Do I need to make a transfer? (man ⇔)	ha'im ani tsariχ la'asot haχlafa? האם אני צריך לעשות החלפה?
Do I need to make a transfer? (woman ⇔)	ha'im ani tsriχa la'asot haχlafa? האם אני צריכה לעשות החלפה?

Buying tickets

Where can I buy tickets?	heiχan efʃar liknot kartisim? היכן אפשר לקנות כרטיסים?
ticket	kartis כרטיס
to buy a ticket	liknot kartis לקנות כרטיס
ticket price	meχir kartis מחיר כרטיס
Where to?	le'an? לאן?
To what station?	le''eizo taχana? לאיזו תחנה?
I need … (man ⊲)	ani tsariχ … אני צריך …
I need … (woman ⊲)	ani tsriχa … אני צריכה …
one ticket	kartis eχad כרטיס אחד
two tickets	ʃnei kartisim שני כרטיסים
three tickets	ʃloʃa kartisim שלושה כרטיסים
one-way	kivun eχad כיוון אחד
round-trip	haloχ vaʃov הלוך ושוב
first class	maχlaka riʃona מחלקה ראשונה
second class	maχlaka ʃniya מחלקה שנייה
today	hayom היום
tomorrow	maχar מחר
the day after tomorrow	maχara'tayim מחרתיים
in the morning	ba'boker בבוקר
in the afternoon	aχar hatsaha'rayim אחר הצהריים
in the evening	ba''erev בערב

aisle seat

moʃav bama'avar
מושב במעבר

window seat

moʃav leyad haχalon
מושב ליד החלון

How much?

kama?
כמה?

Can I pay by credit card?

ha'im efʃar leʃalem bekatrtis aʃrai?
האם אפשר לשלם בכרטיס אשראי?

Bus

bus	'otobus
	אוטובוס
intercity bus	'otobus bein ironi
	אוטובוס בין-עירוני
bus stop	taχanat 'otobus
	תחנת אוטובוס
Where's the nearest bus stop?	eifo taχanat ha''otobus hakrova beyoter?
	איפה תחנת האוטובוס הקרובה ביותר?
number (bus ~, etc.)	mispar
	מספר
Which bus do I take to get to …?	eize 'otobus tsariχ la'kaχat kedei leha'gi'a le …?
	איזה אוטובוס צריך לקחת כדי להגיע ל …?
Does this bus go to …?	ha'im ha''otobus haze ma'gi'a le …?
	האם האוטובוס הזה מגיע ל …?
How frequent are the buses?	ma hatadirut ʃel ha'oto'busim?
	מה התדירות של האוטובוסים?
every 15 minutes	kol χameʃ esre dakot
	כל חמש עשרה דקות
every half hour	kol χatsi ʃa'a
	כל חצי שעה
every hour	kol ʃa'a
	כל שעה
several times a day	mispar pe'amim beyom
	מספר פעמים ביום
… times a day	… pe'amim beyom
	… פעמים ביום
schedule	luaχ zmanim
	לוח זמנים
Where can I see the schedule?	heiχan efʃar lir'ot et 'luaχ hazmanim?
	היכן אפשר לראות את לוח הזמנים?
When is the next bus?	matai ha''otobus haba?
	מתי האוטובוס הבא?
When is the first bus?	matai ha''otobus hariʃon?
	מתי האוטובוס הראשון?
When is the last bus?	matai ha''otobus ha'aχaron?
	מתי האוטובוס האחרון?

stop	taχanat atsira
	תחנת עצירה
next stop	hataχana haba'a
	התחנה הבאה
last stop (terminus)	taχana aχrona
	תחנה אחרונה
Stop here, please. (⇨ man)	atsor kan, bevakaʃa.
	עצור כאן, בבקשה.
Stop here, please. (⇨ woman)	itsri kan, bevakaʃa.
	עצרי כאן, בבקשה.
Excuse me, this is my stop. (⇨ man)	slaχ li, zo hataχana ʃeli.
	סלח לי, זו התחנה שלי.
Excuse me, this is my stop. (⇨ woman)	silχi li, zo hataχana ʃeli.
	סלחי לי, זו התחנה שלי.

Train

train	ra'kevet
	רכבת
suburban train	ra'kevet parvarim
	רכבת פרברים
long-distance train	ra'kevet bein ironit
	רכבת בין-עירונית
train station	taχanat ra'kevet
	תחנת רכבת
Excuse me, where is the exit to the platform? (⇨ man)	slaχ li, 'eifo hayetsi'a laratsif?
	סלח לי, איפה היציאה לרציף?
Excuse me, where is the exit to the platform? (⇨ woman)	silχi li, 'eifo hayetsi'a laratsif?
	סלחי לי, איפה היציאה לרציף?

Does this train go to …?	ha'im hara'kevet hazo megi'a le …?
	האם הרכבת הזו מגיעה ל …?
next train	hara'kevet haba'a
	הרכבת הבאה
When is the next train?	matai hara'kevet haba'a?
	מתי הרכבת הבאה?
Where can I see the schedule?	heiχan efʃar lir'ot et 'luaχ hazmanim?
	היכן אפשר לראות את לוח הזמנים?
From which platform?	me"eize ratsif?
	מאיזה רציף?
When does the train arrive in …?	matai hara'kevet megi'a le …?
	מתי הרכבת מגיעה ל …?

Please help me. (⇨ man)	azor li bevakaʃa.
	עזור לי בבקשה.
Please help me. (⇨ woman)	izri li bevakaʃa.
	עזרי לי בבקשה.
I'm looking for my seat. (man ⇨)	ani meχapes et hamoʃav ʃeli.
	אני מחפש את המושב שלי.
I'm looking for my seat. (woman ⇨)	ani meχa'peset et hamoʃav ʃeli.
	אני מחפשת את המושב שלי.
We're looking for our seats. (couple , men ⇨)	anu meχapsim et hamoʃavim ʃe'lanu
	אנו מחפשים את המושבים שלנו.
We're looking for our seats. (women ⇨)	anu meχapsot et hamoʃavim ʃe'lanu
	אנו מחפשות את המושבים שלנו.
My seat is taken.	hamoʃav ʃeli tafus.
	המושב שלי תפוס.
Our seats are taken.	hamoʃavim ʃe'lanu tfusim.
	המושבים שלנו תפוסים.
I'm sorry but this is my seat. (man ⇨)	ani mitsta'er, aval ze hamoʃav ʃeli.
	אני מצטער, אבל זה המושב שלי.

I'm sorry but this is my seat. (woman ⇨)

ani mitsta"eret, aval ze hamoʃav ʃeli.
אני מצטערת, אבל זה המושב שלי.

Is this seat taken?

ha'im hamoʃav haze tafus?
האם המושב הזה תפוס?

May I sit here? (man ⇨)

ha'im ani yaχol la'ʃevet kan?
האם אני יכול לשבת כאן?

May I sit here? (woman ⇨)

ha'im ani yeχola laʃevet kan?
האם אני יכולה לשבת כאן?

On the train. Dialogue (No ticket)

Ticket, please.	kartis, bevakaʃa. כרטיס, בבקשה.
I don't have a ticket.	ein li kartis. אין לי כרטיס.
I lost my ticket.	i'badti et hakartis ʃeli. איבדתי את הכרטיס שלי.
I forgot my ticket at home.	ʃa'χaχti et hakartis ʃeli ba'bayit שכחתי את הכרטיס שלי בבית.
You can buy a ticket from me. (⇨ man)	ata yaχol liknot kartis mi'meni. אתה יכול לקנות כרטיס ממני.
You can buy a ticket from me. (⇨ woman)	at yeχola liknot kartis mi'meni. את יכולה לקנות כרטיס ממני.
You will also have to pay a fine. (⇨ man)	titstareχ gam leʃalem knas. תצטרך גם לשלם קנס.
You will also have to pay a fine. (⇨ woman)	titstarχi gam leʃalem knas. תצטרכי גם לשלם קנס.
Okay.	okei. אוקיי.
Where are you going? (⇨ man)	le'an ata no'se'a? לאן אתה נוסע?
Where are you going? (⇨ woman)	le'an at nos'a'at? לאן את נוסעת?
I'm going to … (man ⇨)	ani no'se'a le… אני נוסע ל...
I'm going to … (woman ⇨)	ani nos'a'at le… אני נוסעת ל...
How much? I don't understand. (man ⇨)	kama? ani lo mevin. כמה? אני לא מבין.
How much? I don't understand. (woman ⇨)	kama? ani lo mevina. כמה? אני לא מבינה.
Write it down, please. (⇨ man)	ktov li et ze, bevakaʃa. כתוב לי את זה, בבקשה.
Write it down, please. (⇨ woman)	kitvi li et ze, bevakaʃa. כתבי לי את זה, בבקשה.
Okay. Can I pay with a credit card?	okei. ha'im efʃar leʃalem bekartis aʃrai? אוקיי. האם אפשר לשלם בכרטיס אשראי?
Yes, you can.	ken, efʃar. כן, אפשר.
Here's your receipt. (⇨ man)	hine hakabala ʃelχa. הנה הקבלה שלך.
Here's your receipt. (⇨ woman)	hine hakabala ʃelaχ' הינה הקבלה שלך

Sorry about the fine. (man ☞)

ani mitsta'er be'kefer laknas.
אני מצטער בקשר לקנס.

Sorry about the fine. (woman ☞)

ani mitsta"eret be'kefer laknas.
אני מצטערת בקשר לקנס.

That's okay. It was my fault.

ze be'seder. zo afmati.
זה בסדר. זו אשמתי.

Enjoy your trip.

tiyul mehane.
טיול מהנה.

Taxi

taxi	monit
	מונית
taxi driver (masc.)	nahag monit
	נהג מונית
taxi driver (fem.)	na'heget monit
	נהגת מונית
to catch a taxi	litpos monit
	לתפוס מונית
taxi stand	taχanat moniyot
	תחנת מוניות
Where can I get a taxi?	eifo efʃar la'kaχat monit?
	איפה אפשר לקחת מונית?

to call a taxi	lehazmin monit
	להזמין מונית
I need a taxi. (man ⇨)	ani tsariχ monit
	אני צריך מונית
I need a taxi. (woman ⇨)	ani tsriχa monit
	אני צריכה מונית
Right now.	aχʃav.
	עכשיו.
What is your address (location)? (⇨ man)	ma ha'ktovet ʃelχa?
	מה הכתובת שלך?
What is your address (location)? (⇨ woman)	ma ha'ktovet ʃelaχ?
	מה הכתובת שלך?
My address is ...	ha'ktovet ʃeli hi ...
	הכתובת שלי היא ...
Your destination? (⇨ man)	le'an ata no'se'a?
	לאן אתה נוסע?
Your destination? (⇨ woman)	le'an at nos'a'at?
	לאן את נוסעת?

Excuse me, ... (⇨ man)	slaχ li, ...
	סלח לי, ...
Excuse me, ... (⇨ woman)	silχi li, ...
	סלחי לי, ...
Are you available? (⇨ man)	ha'im ata panui?
	האם אתה פנוי?
Are you available? (⇨ woman)	ha'im at pnuya?
	האם את פנויה?
How much is it to get to ...?	kama ze ole lin'so'a le ...?
	כמה זה עולה לנסוע ל...?
Do you know where it is? (⇨ man)	ha'im ata yo'de'a 'eifo ze?
	האם אתה יודע איפה זה?

Do you know where it is? (⇨ woman)	ha'im at yod'a'at 'eifo ze? האם את יודעת איפה זה?
Airport, please.	lisde hate'ufa, bevakaʃa. לשדה התעופה, בבקשה.
Stop here, please. (⇨ man)	atsor kan, bevakaʃa. עצור כאן, בבקשה.
Stop here, please. (⇨ woman)	itsri kan, bevakaʃa. עצרי כאן, בבקשה.
It's not here.	ze lo kan. זה לא כאן.
This is the wrong address.	zo lo ha'ktovet hanexona. זו לא הכתובת הנכונה.
Turn left. (⇨ man)	pne 'smola. פנה שמאלה.
Turn left. (⇨ woman)	pni 'smola. פני שמאלה.
Turn right. (⇨ man)	pne ya'mina. פנה ימינה.
Turn right. (⇨ woman)	pni ya'mina. פני ימינה.

How much do I owe you? (man ⇨)	kama me'gi'a lexa? כמה מגיע לך?
How much do I owe you? (woman ⇨)	kama me'gi'a lax? כמה מגיע לך?
I'd like a receipt, please.	efʃar lekabel kabala, bevakaʃa? אפשר לקבל קבלה, בבקשה?
Keep the change. (⇨ man)	ʃmor et ha''odef. שמור את העודף.
Keep the change. (⇨ woman)	ʃimri et ha''odef. שמרי את העודף.

Would you please wait for me? (⇨ man)	ha'im ata muxan lexakot li, bevakaʃa? האם אתה מוכן לחכות לי, בבקשה?
Would you please wait for me? (⇨ woman)	ha'im at muxana lexakot li, bevakaʃa? האם את מוכנה לחכות לי, בבקשה?
five minutes	xameʃ dakot חמש דקות
ten minutes	eser dakot עשר דקות
fifteen minutes	xameʃ esre dakot חמש עשרה דקות
twenty minutes	esrim dakot עשרים דקות
half an hour	xatsi ʃa'a חצי שעה

Hotel

Hello.	ʃalom.
	שלום.
My name is ...	kor'im li ...
	... קוראים לי
I have a reservation.	yeʃ li hazmana.
	יש לי הזמנה.

I need ... (man ☺)	ani tsariҳ ...
	... אני צריך
I need ... (woman ☺)	ani tsriҳa ...
	... אני צריכה
a single room	ҳeder leyaҳid
	חדר ליחיד
a double room	ҳeder zugi
	חדר זוגי
How much is that?	kama ze ole?
	?במה זה עולה
That's a bit expensive.	ze ktsat yakar.
	זה קצת יקר.

Do you have anything else? (☺ man)	ha'im yeʃ leҳa 'optsiyot aҳerot?
	?האם יש לך אופציות אחרות
Do you have anything else? (☺ woman)	ha'im yeʃ laҳ 'optsiyot aҳerot?
	?האם יש לך אופציות אחרות
I'll take it.	ani ekaҳ et ze.
	אני אקח את זה.
I'll pay in cash.	ani eʃalem bimzuman.
	אני אשלם במזומן.

I've got a problem.	yeʃ li be'aya.
	יש לי בעיה.
My ... is broken. (masc.)	ha... ʃeli mekulkal.
	ה... שלי מקולקל.
My ... is broken. (fem.)	ha... ʃeli mekul'kelet.
	ה... שלי מקולקלת.
My ... is out of order. (masc.)	ha... ʃeli lo oved.
	ה... שלי לא עובד.
My ... is out of order. (fem.)	ha... ʃeli lo o'vedet.
	ה... שלי לא עובדת.
TV	tele'vizya
	טלוויזיה
air conditioner	mizug avir
	מיזוג אוויר

tap	berez ברז
shower	mik'laχat מקלחת
sink	kiyor כיור
safe	ka'sefet כספת
door lock	man'ul מנעול
electrical outlet	ʃeka שקע
hairdryer	meyabeʃ se'ar מייבש שיער

I don't have …	ein li … אין לי ...
water	mayim מים
light	te'ura תאורה
electricity	χaʃmal חשמל

Can you give me …?	ha'im at yeχola latet li …? האם את יכולה לתת לי ...?
a towel	ma'gevet מגבת
a blanket	smiχa שמיכה
slippers	na'alei 'bayit נעלי בית
a robe	χaluk חלוק
shampoo	ʃampo שמפו
soap	sabon סבון

I'd like to change rooms. (man ⇨)	ani rotse lehaχlif 'χeder. אני רוצה להחליף חדר.
I'd like to change rooms. (woman ⇨)	ani rotsa lehaχlif 'χeder. אני רוצה להחליף חדר.
I can't find my key. (man ⇨)	ani lo motse et hamaf'teaχ ʃeli. אני לא מוצא את המפתח שלי.
I can't find my key. (woman ⇨)	ani lo motset et hamaf'teaχ ʃeli. אני לא מוצאת את המפתח שלי.
Could you open my room, please?	ha'im ata yaχol lif'toaχ et χadri, bevakaʃa? האם אתה יכול לפתוח את חדרי, בבקשה?

Who's there?	mi ʃam? מי שם?
Come in!	hikanes! היכנס!
Just a minute!	rak 'rega! רק רגע!
Not right now, please.	lo axʃav, bevakaʃa. לא עכשיו, בבקשה.

Come to my room, please.	bo'i lexadri, bevakaʃa. בואי לחדרי, בבקשה.
I'd like to order food service. (man ⇨)	ani mevakeʃ lehazmin ʃerut xadarim. אני מבקש להזמין שירות חדרים.
I'd like to order food service. (woman ⇨)	ani meva'keʃet lehazmin ʃerut xadarim. אני מבקשת להזמין שירות חדרים.
My room number is …	mispar ha'xeder ʃeli hu … מספר החדר שלי הוא ...

I'm leaving … (man ⇨)	ani ozev … אני עוזב ...
I'm leaving … (woman ⇨)	ani o'zevet … אני עוזבת ...
We're leaving … (couple , men ⇨)	a'naxnu ozvim … אנחנו עוזבים ...
We're leaving … (women ⇨)	a'naxnu ozvot … אנחנו עוזבות ...

right now	axʃav עכשיו
this afternoon	axar hatsaha'rayim אחר הצהריים
tonight	ha'laila הלילה
tomorrow	maxar מחר
tomorrow morning	maxar ba'boker מחר בבוקר
tomorrow evening	maxar ba''erev מחר בערב
the day after tomorrow	maxara'tayim מחרתיים

I'd like to pay. (man ⇨)	ani rotse leʃalem. אני רוצה לשלם.
I'd like to pay. (woman ⇨)	ani rotsa leʃalem. אני רוצה לשלם.
Everything was wonderful.	hakol haya nehedar. הכל היה נהדר.
Where can I get a taxi?	eifo efʃar la'kaxat monit? איפה אפשר לקחת מונית?

Would you call a taxi for me, please?
(⇨ man)

ha'im ata yaχol lehazmin li monit,
bevakaʃa?
**האם אתה יכול להזמין לי מונית,
בבקשה?**

Would you call a taxi for me, please?
(⇨ woman)

ha'im at yeχola lehazmin li monit,
bevakaʃa?
**האם את יכולה להזמין לי מונית,
בבקשה?**

Restaurant

Can I look at the menu, please?	ha'im efʃar lekabel tafrit, bevakaʃa? האם אפשר לקבל תפריט, בבקשה?
Table for one.	ʃulχan leyaχid. שולחן ליחיד.
There are two (three, four) of us.	a'naχnu 'ʃnayim (ʃloʃa, arba'a). אנחנו שניים (שלושה, ארבעה).

Smoking	me'aʃnim מעשנים
No smoking	lo me'aʃnim לא מעשנים
Excuse me! (addressing a waiter) (⊹ man)	slaχ li! סלח לי!
Excuse me! (addressing a waiter) (⊹ woman)	silχi li! סלחי לי!
menu	tafrit תפריט
wine list	reʃimat yeinot רשימת יינות
The menu, please.	tafrit, bevakaʃa. תפריט, בבקשה.

Are you ready to order? (⊹ man)	ha'im ata muχan lehazmin? האם אתה מוכן להזמין?
Are you ready to order? (⊹ woman)	ha'im at muχana lehazmin? האם את מוכנה להזמין?
What will you have? (⊹ man)	ma tirtse? מה תרצה?
What will you have? (⊹ woman)	ma tirtsi? מה תרצי?
I'll have ... (man ⊹)	ani rotse ... אני רוצה ...
I'll have ... (woman ⊹)	ani rotsa ... אני רוצה ...
I'm a vegetarian. (man ⊹)	ani tsimχoni. אני צמחוני.
I'm a vegetarian. (woman ⊹)	ani tsimχonit. אני צמחונית.
meat	basar בשר
fish	dagim דגים
vegetables	yerakot ירקות

Do you have vegetarian dishes?

ha'im yeʃ laχem manot tsimχoniyot?
האם יש לכם מנות צמחוניות?

I don't eat pork. (man ⇨)

ani lo oχel χazir.
אני לא אוכל חזיר.

I don't eat pork. (woman ⇨)

ani lo o'χelet χazir.
אני לא אוכלת חזיר.

He doesn't eat meat.

hu lo oχel basar.
הוא לא אוכל בשר.

She doesn't eat meat.

hi lo o'χelet basar.
היא לא אוכלת בשר.

I am allergic to … (man ⇨)

ani a'lergi le…
אני אלרגי ל...

I am allergic to … (woman ⇨)

ani a'lergit le…
אני אלרגית ל...

Would you please bring me … (⇦ man)

ha'im ata yaχol lehavi li, bevakaʃa, …
האם אתה יכול להביא לי, בבקשה, ...

Would you please bring me … (⇦ woman)

ha'im at yeχola lehavi li, bevakaʃa, …
האם את יכולה להביא לי, בבקשה, ...

salt | pepper | sugar

melaχ | 'pilpel | sukar
מלח | פלפל | סוכר

coffee | tea | dessert

kafe | te | ki'nuaχ
קפה | תה | קינוח

water | sparkling | plain

mayim | mugazim | regilim
מים | מוגזים| רגילים

a spoon | fork | knife

kaf | mazleg | sakin
כף | מזלג | סכין

a plate | napkin

tsa'laχat | mapit
צלחת | מפית

Enjoy your meal!

bete'avon!
בתיאבון!

One more, please.

od eχad /aχat/, bevakaʃa.
עוד אחד /אחת/, בבקשה.

It was very delicious.

ze haya me'od ta'im.
זה היה מאוד טעים.

---

check | change | tip

χeʃbon | 'odef | tip
חשבון | עודף | טיפ

Check, please.
(Could I have the check, please?)

χeʃbon, bevakaʃa.
חשבון, בבקשה.

Can I pay by credit card?

ha'im efʃar leʃalem bekatrtis aʃrai?
האם אפשר לשלם בכרטיס אשראי?

I'm sorry, there's a mistake here.
(man ⇨)

ani mitsta'er, yeʃ kan ta'ut.
אני מצטער, יש כאן טעות.

I'm sorry, there's a mistake here.
(woman ⇨)

ani mitsta"eret, yeʃ kan ta'ut.
אני מצטערת, יש כאן טעות.

Shopping

Can I help you? (⇨ man)
ha'im efʃar la'azor leχa?
האם אפשר לעזור לך?

Can I help you? (⇨ woman)
ha'im efʃar la'azor laχ?
האם אפשר לעזור לך?

Do you have ...?
ha'im yeʃ laχem ...?
האם יש לכם ...?

I'm looking for ... (man ⇨)
ani meχapes ...
אני מחפש ...

I'm looking for ... (woman ⇨)
ani meχa'peset ...
אני מחפשת ...

I need ... (man ⇨)
ani tsariχ ...
אני צריך ...

I need ... (woman ⇨)
ani tsriχa ...
אני צריכה ...

I'm just looking. (man ⇨)
ani rak mistakel.
אני רק מסתכל.

I'm just looking. (woman ⇨)
ani rak mista'kelet.
אני רק מסתכלת.

We're just looking. (couple , men ⇨)
a'naχnu rak mistaklim.
אנחנו רק מסתכלים.

We're just looking. (women ⇨)
a'naχnu rak mistaklot.
אנחנו רק מסתכלות.

I'll come back later.
ani aχazor me'uχar yoter.
אני אחזור מאוחר יותר.

We'll come back later.
a'naχnu naχazor me'uχar yoter.
אנחנו נחזור מאוחר יותר.

discounts | sale
hanaχot | mivtsa
הנחות | מבצע

Would you please show me ... (⇨ man)
ha'im ata yaχol lehar'ot li ...
האם אתה יכול להראות לי ...

Would you please show me ... (⇨ woman)
ha'im at yeχola lehar'ot li ...
האם את יכולה להראות לי ...

Would you please give me ... (⇨ man)
ha'im ata yaχol latet li, bevakaʃa ...
האם אתה יכול לתת לי, בבקשה ...

Would you please give me ... (⇨ woman)
ha'im at yeχola latet li, bevakaʃa ...
האם את יכולה לתת לי, בבקשה ...

Can I try it on? (man ⇨)
ha'im ani yaχol limdod et ze?
האם אני יכול למדוד את זה?

Can I try it on? (woman ⇨)
ha'im ani yeχola limdod et ze?
האם אני יכולה למדוד את זה?

Excuse me, where's the fitting room?
(⇨ man)

slaχ li, 'eifo χadar hahalbaʃa?
סלח לי, איפה חדר ההלבשה?

Excuse me, where's the fitting room?
(⇨ woman)

silχi li, 'eifo χadar hahalbaʃa?
סלחי לי, איפה חדר ההלבשה?

Which color would you like? (⇨ man)

eize 'tseva ha'yita rotse?
איזה צבע היית רוצה?

Which color would you like? (⇨ woman)

eize 'tseva hayit rotsa?
איזה צבע היית רוצה?

size | length

mida | 'oreχ
מידה | אורך

How does it fit? (⇨ man)

ha'im ze mat'im leχa?
האם זה מתאים לך?

How does it fit? (⇨ woman)

ha'im ze mat'im laχ?
האם זה מתאים לך?

How much is it?

kama ze ole?
כמה זה עולה?

That's too expensive.

ze yakar midai.
זה יקר מידי.

I'll take it.

ani ekaχ et ze.
אני אקח את זה.

Excuse me, where do I pay? (man ⇨)

slaχ li, 'eifo meʃalmim?
סלח לי, איפה משלמים?

Excuse me, where do I pay? (woman ⇨)

silχi li, 'eifo 'meʃalmim?
סלחי לי, איפה משלמים?

Will you pay in cash or credit card?
(⇨ man)

ha'im ata meʃalem bimzuman
o bekartis aʃrai?
האם אתה משלם במזומן
או בברטיס אשראי?

Will you pay in cash or credit card?
(⇨ woman)

ha'im at meʃa'lemet bimzuman
o bekartis aʃrai?
האם את משלמת במזומן
או בברטיס אשראי?

In cash | with credit card

bimzuman | bekartis aʃrai
במזומן | בכרטיס אשראי

Do you want the receipt? (⇨ man)

ha'im ata rotse et hakabala?
האם אתה רוצה את הקבלה?

Do you want the receipt? (⇨ woman)

ha'im at rotsa et hakabala?
האם את רוצה את הקבלה?

Yes, please.

ken, bevakaʃa.
כן, בבקשה.

No, it's OK.

lo, ze be'seder.
לא, זה בסדר.

Thank you. Have a nice day! (⇨ man)

toda. ʃeyihye leχa yom na'im!
תודה. שיהיה לך יום נעים!

Thank you. Have a nice day! (⇨ woman)

toda. ʃeyihye laχ yom na'im!
תודה. שיהיה לך יום נעים!

In town

Excuse me, please. (⇨ man)	slaχ li, bevakaʃa. סלח לי, בבקשה.
Excuse me, please. (⇨ woman)	silχi li, bevakaʃa. סלחי לי, בבקשה.
I'm looking for ... (man ⇨)	ani meχapes ... אני מחפש ...
I'm looking for ... (woman ⇨)	ani meχa'peset ... אני מחפשת ...
the subway	ra'kevet taχtit רכבת תחתית
my hotel	et hamalon ʃeli את המלון שלי
the movie theater	et hakol'no'a את הקולנוע
a taxi stand	taχanat moniyot תחנת מוניות

an ATM	kaspomat כספומט
a foreign exchange office	misrad mat'be'a χuts משרד מטבע חוץ
an internet café	beit kafe 'internet בית קפה אינטרנט
... street	reχov ... רחוב ...
this place	hamakom haze המקום הזה

Do you know where ... is? (⇨ man)	ha'im ata yo'de'a heiχan nimtsa ...? האם אתה יודע היכן נמצא ...?
Do you know where ... is? (⇨ woman)	ha'im at yo'da'at heiχan nimtsa ...? האם את יודעת היכן נמצא ...?
Which street is this?	eize reχov ze? איזה רחוב זה?
Show me where we are right now. (⇨ man)	har'e li heiχan 'anu nimtsa'im aχʃav. הראה לי היכן אנו נמצאים עכשיו.
Show me where we are right now. (⇨ woman)	har'i li heiχan anu nimtsa'im aχʃav. הראי לי היכן אנו נמצאים עכשיו.
Can I get there on foot?	ha'im efʃar leha'gi'a leʃam ba'regel? האם אפשר להגיע לשם ברגל?
Do you have a map of the city? (⇨ man)	ha'im yeʃ leχa mapa ʃel ha'ir? האם יש לך מפה של העיר?
Do you have a map of the city? (⇨ woman)	ha'im yeʃ laχ mapa ʃel ha'ir? האם יש לך מפה של העיר?

How much is a ticket to get in?

kama ole kartis knisa?
כמה עולה כרטיס כניסה?

Can I take pictures here?

ha'im mutar letsalem kan?
האם מותר לצלם כאן?

Are you open?

ha'im atem ptuxim?
האם אתם פתוחים?

When do you open?

matai atem potxim?
מתי אתם פותחים?

When do you close?

matai atem sogrim?
מתי אתם סוגרים?

Money

money	kesef
	כסף
cash	mezuman
	מזומן
paper money	ſtarot 'kesef
	שטרות כסף
loose change	kesef katan
	כסף קטן
check | change | tip	xeſbon | 'odef | tip
	חשבון | עודף | טיפ

credit card	kartis aſrai
	כרטיס אשראי
wallet	arnak
	ארנק
to buy	liknot
	לקנות
to pay	leſalem
	לשלם
fine	knas
	קנס
free	xinam
	חינם

Where can I buy ...?	eifo efſar liknot ...?
	איפה אפשר לקנות ...?
Is the bank open now?	ha'im ha'bank pa'tuax axſav?
	האם הבנק פתוח עכשיו?
When does it open?	matai ze nisgar?
	מתי זה נפתח?
When does it close?	matai ze niftax?
	מתי זה נסגר?

How much?	kama?
	כמה?
How much is this?	kama ze ole?
	כמה זה עולה?
That's too expensive.	ze yakar midai.
	זה יקר מידי.

Excuse me, where do I pay?	slixa, 'eifo meſalmim?
	סליחה, איפה משלמים?
Check, please.	xeſbon, bevakaſa.
	חשבון, בבקשה.

Can I pay by credit card?

ha'im eʃʃar leʃalem bekatrtis aʃrai?
האם אפשר לשלם בכרטיס אשראי?

Is there an ATM here?

ha'im yeʃ kan kaspomat?
האם יש כאן כספומט?

I'm looking for an ATM. (man ⇨)

ani meχapes kaspomat.
אני מחפש בספומט.

I'm looking for an ATM. (woman ⇨)

ani meχa'peset kaspomat.
אני מחפשת בספומט.

I'm looking for a foreign exchange office. (man ⇨)

ani meχapes misrad mat'be'a χuts.
אני מחפש משרד מטבע חוץ.

I'm looking for a foreign exchange office. (woman ⇨)

ani meχa'peset misrad mat'be'a χuts.
אני מחפשת משרד מטבע חוץ.

I'd like to change ... (man ⇨)

ani rotse lehaχlif ...
אני רוצה להחליף ...

I'd like to change ... (woman ⇨)

ani rotsa lehaχlif ...
אני רוצה להחליף ...

What is the exchange rate?

ma 'ʃa'ar haχalifin?
מה שער החליפין?

Do you need my passport? (⇦ man)

ha'im ata tsariχ et hadarkon ʃeli?
האם אתה צריך את הדרכון שלי?

Do you need my passport? (⇦ woman)

ha'im at tsriχa et hadarkon ʃeli?
האם את צריכה את הדרכון שלי?

Time

What time is it?	ma haʃa'a? מה השעה?
When?	matai? מתי?
At what time?	be''eizo ʃa'a? באיזו שעה?
now | later | after …	aχʃav | aχar kaχ | aχrei … עכשיו | אחר כך | אחרי ...

one o'clock	aχat אחת
one fifteen	aχat va'reva אחת ורבע
one thirty	aχat va'χetsi אחת וחצי
one forty-five	aχat arba'im veχameʃ אחת ארבעים וחמש

one | two | three	aχat | ʃ'tayim | ʃaloʃ אחת | שתיים | שלוש
four | five | six	arba | χameʃ | ʃeʃ ארבע | חמש | שש
seven | eight | nine	ʃeva | 'ʃmone | 'teʃa שבע | שמונה | תשע
ten | eleven | twelve	eser | aχat esre | ʃtem esre עשר | אחת עשרה | שתים עשרה

in …	toχ … תוך ...
five minutes	χameʃ dakot חמש דקות
ten minutes	eser dakot עשר דקות
fifteen minutes	χameʃ esre dakot חמש עשרה דקות
twenty minutes	esrim dakot עשרים דקות

half an hour	χatsi ʃa'a חצי שעה
an hour	ʃa'a שעה

in the morning	ba'boker
	בבוקר
early in the morning	mukdam ba'boker, haʃkem ba'boker
	מוקדם בבוקר, השכם בבוקר
this morning	ha'boker
	הבוקר
tomorrow morning	maχar ba'boker
	מחר בבוקר

in the middle of the day	batsaha'rayim
	בצהריים
in the afternoon	aχar hatsaha'rayim
	אחר הצהריים
in the evening	ba''erev
	בערב
tonight	ha'laila
	הלילה

at night	ba'laila
	בלילה
yesterday	etmol
	אתמול
today	hayom
	היום
tomorrow	maχar
	מחר
the day after tomorrow	maχara'tayim
	מחרתיים

What day is it today?	eize yom hayom?
	?איזה יום היום
It's …	hayom …
	… היום
Monday	yom ʃeni
	יום שני
Tuesday	yom ʃliʃi
	יום שלישי
Wednesday	yom revi'i
	יום רביעי

Thursday	yom χamiʃi
	יום חמישי
Friday	yom ʃiʃi
	יום שישי
Saturday	ʃabat
	שבת
Sunday	yom riʃon
	יום ראשון

Greetings. Introductions

Pleased to meet you. (man ⇨ man)
ani sameaχ lehakir otχa.
אני שמח להכיר אותך.

Pleased to meet you. (man ⇨ woman)
ani sameaχ lehakir otaχ.
אני שמח להכיר אותך.

Pleased to meet you. (woman ⇨ man)
ani smeχa lifgoʃ otχa.
אני שמחה לפגוש אותך.

Pleased to meet you. (woman ⇨ woman)
ani smeχa lifgoʃ otaχ.
אני שמחה לפגוש אותך.

Hello.
ʃalom.
שלום.

Me too.
gam ani.
גם אני.

I'd like you to meet ... (man ⇨ man)
ha'yiti rotse ʃetakir et ...
הייתי רוצה שתכיר את ...

I'd like you to meet ... (man ⇨ woman)
ha'yiti rotse ʃeta'kiri et ...
הייתי רוצה שתכירי את ...

I'd like you to meet ... (woman ⇨ man)
ha'yiti rotsa ʃetakir et ...
הייתי רוצה שתכיר את ...

I'd like you to meet ... (woman ⇨ woman)
ha'yiti rotsa ʃeta'kiri et ...
הייתי רוצה שתכירי את ...

Nice to meet you. (⇨ man)
na'im lifgoʃ otχa.
נעים לפגוש אותך.

Nice to meet you. (⇨ woman)
na'im lifgoʃ otaχ.
נעים לפגוש אותך.

How are you? (⇨ man)
ma ʃlomχa?
מה שלומך?

How are you? (⇨ woman)
ma ʃlomeχ?
מה שלומך?

My name is ...
kor'im li ...
קוראים לי ...

His name is ...
kor'im lo ...
קוראים לו ...

Her name is ...
kor'im la ...
קוראים לה ...

What's your name? (⇨ man)
eiχ kor'im leχa?
איך קוראים לך?

What's your name? (⇨ woman)
eiχ kor'im laχ?
איך קוראים לך?

What's his name?
eiχ kor'im lo?
איך קוראים לו?

What's her name?
eiχ kor'im la?
איך קוראים לה?

What's your last name? (⇨ man)	ma ʃem hamiʃpaxa ʃelxa?
	?מה שם המשפחה שלך
What's your last name? (⇨ woman)	ma ʃem hamiʃpaxa ʃelax?
	?מה שם המשפחה שלך
You can call me … (⇨ man)	ata yaxol likro li …
	... אתה יבול לקרוא לי
You can call me … (⇨ woman)	at yexola likro li …
	... את יבולה לקרוא לי
Where are you from? (⇨ man)	me"eifo ata?
	?מאיפה אתה
Where are you from? (⇨ woman)	me"eifo at?
	?מאיפה את

I'm from …	ani mi…
	...אני מ
What do you do for a living? (⇨ man)	bema ata oved?
	?במה אתה עובד
What do you do for a living? (⇨ woman)	bema at o'vedet?
	?במה את עובדת

Who is this? (masc.)	mi ze?
	?מי זה
Who is this? (fem.)	mi zo?
	?מי זו
Who is he?	mi ze?
	?מי זה
Who is she?	mi zo?
	?מי זו
Who are they?	mi 'ele?
	?מי אלה

This is …	ze …
	... זה
my friend (masc.)	xaver ʃeli
	חבר שלי
my husband	ba'ali
	בעלי
my father	avi
	אבי
my brother	axi
	אחי
my son	bni
	בני

This is …	zo …
	... זו
my friend (fem.)	xavera ʃeli
	חברה שלי
my wife	iʃti
	אשתי
my mother	immi
	אמי

my sister	aχoti
	אחותי
my daughter	biti
	בתי

This is our son.	ze haben ʃe'lanu.
	זה הבן שלנו.
This is our daughter.	zo habat ʃe'lanu.
	זו הבת שלנו.
These are my children.	ele hayeladim ʃeli.
	אלה הילדים שלי.
These are our children.	ele hayeladim ʃe'lanu.
	אלה הילדים שלנו.

Farewells

Good bye!	ʃalom! שלום!
Bye! (inform.)	bai! ביי!
See you tomorrow.	lehitra'ot maxar. להתראות מחר.
See you soon.	lehitra'ot bekarov. להתראות בקרוב.
See you at seven.	lehitra'ot be'ʃeva. להתראות בשבע.
Have fun!	asu xayim! עשו חיים!
Talk to you later.	lehiʃta'me'a. להשתמע.
Have a nice weekend.	sof ʃa'vu'a na'im. סוף שבוע נעים.
Good night.	laila tov. לילה טוב.
It's time for me to go.	hi'gi'a zmani la'leχet. הגיע זמני ללכת.
I have to go. (man ⇨)	ani xayav la'leχet. אני חייב ללכת.
I have to go. (woman ⇨)	ani xa'yevet la'leχet. אני חייבת ללכת.
I will be right back.	ani axazor miyad. אני אחזור מייד.
It's late.	kvar me'uχar. כבר מאוחר.
I have to get up early. (man ⇨)	ani tsariχ lakum mukdam. אני צריך לקום מוקדם.
I have to get up early. (woman ⇨)	ani tsriχa lakum mukdam. אני צריכה לקום מוקדם.
I'm leaving tomorrow. (man ⇨)	ani ozev maχar. אני עוזב מחר.
I'm leaving tomorrow. (woman ⇨)	ani o'zevet maχar. אני עוזבת מחר.
We're leaving tomorrow. (couple , men ⇨)	a'naχnu ozvim maχar. אנחנו עוזבים מחר.
We're leaving tomorrow. (women ⇨)	a'naχnu ozvot maχar. אנחנו עוזבות מחר.

Have a nice trip!	nesi'a tova! !נסיעה טובה
It was nice meeting you. (⇐ man)	haya neχmad lifgoʃ otχa. .היה נחמד לפגוש אותך
It was nice meeting you. (⇐ woman)	haya neχmad lifgoʃ otaχ. .היה נחמד לפגוש אותך
It was nice talking to you. (⇐ man)	haya na'im ledaber itχa. .היה נעים לדבר איתך
It was nice talking to you. (⇐ woman)	haya na'im ledaber itaχ. .היה נעים לדבר איתך
Thanks for everything.	toda al hakol. .תודה על הכל

I had a very good time.	nehe'neti me'od. .נהניתי מאוד
We had a very good time.	nehe'nenu me'od. .נהנינו מאוד
It was really great.	ze haya mamaʃ nehedar. .זה היה ממש נהדר
I'm going to miss you. (⇐ man)	ani etga'a'ge'a e'leχa. .אני אתגעגע אליך
I'm going to miss you. (⇐ woman)	ani etga'a'ge'a e'layiχ. .אני אתגעגע אלייך
We're going to miss you. (⇐ man)	a'naχnu nitga'a'ge'a e'leχa. .אנחנו נתגעגע אליך
We're going to miss you. (⇐ woman)	a'naχnu nitga'a'ge'a e'layiχ. .אנחנו נתגעגע אלייך

Good luck!	behatslaχa! !בהצלחה
Say hi to … (⇐ man)	msor daʃ le… …מסור ד"ש ל
Say hi to … (⇐ woman)	misri daʃ le… …מסרי ד"ש ל

Foreign language

I don't understand. (man ⚬)	ani lo mevin.
	אני לא מבין.
I don't understand. (woman ⚬)	ani lo mevina.
	אני לא מבינה.
Write it down, please. (⚬ man)	ktov li et ze, bevakaʃa.
	כתוב לי את זה, בבקשה.
Write it down, please. (⚬ woman)	kitvi li et ze, bevakaʃa.
	כתבי לי את זה, בבקשה.
Do you speak ...? (⚬ man)	ha'im ata medaber ...?
	?... האם אתה מדבר
Do you speak ...? (⚬ woman)	ha'im at meda'beret ...?
	?... האם את מדברת

I speak a little bit of ... (man ⚬)	ani medaber kʦat ...
	... אני מדבר קצת
I speak a little bit of ... (woman ⚬)	ani meda'beret kʦat ...
	... אני מדברת קצת
English	anglit
	אנגלית
Turkish	turkit
	טורקית
Arabic	aravit
	ערבית
French	ʦarfatit
	צרפתית

German	germanit
	גרמנית
Italian	italkit
	איטלקית
Spanish	sfaradit
	ספרדית
Portuguese	portu'gezit
	פורטוגזית
Chinese	sinit
	סינית
Japanese	ya'panit
	יפנית

Can you repeat that, please. (⚬ man)	ha'im ata yaχol laχazor al ze, bevakaʃa?
	?האם אתה יכול לחזור על זה, בבקשה
Can you repeat that, please. (⚬ woman)	ha'im at yeχola laχazor al ze, bevakaʃa?
	?האם את יכולה לחזור על זה, בבקשה

I understand. (man ☞)	ani mevin. אני מבין.
I understand. (woman ☞)	ani mevina. אני מבינה.
I don't understand. (man ☞)	ani lo mevin. אני לא מבין.
I don't understand. (woman ☞)	ani lo mevina. אני לא מבינה.
Please speak more slowly. (☜ man)	ana daber yoter le'at. אנא דבר יותר לאט.
Please speak more slowly. (☜ woman)	ana dabri yoter le'at. אנא דברי יותר לאט.

| Is that correct? (Am I saying it right?) | ha'im ze naxon?
?האם זה נכון |
| What is this? (What does this mean?) | ma ze?
?מה זה |

Apologies

Excuse me, please. (⇨ man)
slaχ li, bevakaʃa.
סלח לי, בבקשה.

Excuse me, please. (⇨ woman)
silχi li, bevakaʃa.
סלחי לי, בבקשה.

I'm sorry. (man ⇨)
ani mitsta'er.
אני מצטער.

I'm sorry. (woman ⇨)
ani mitsta"eret.
אני מצטערת.

I'm really sorry. (man ⇨)
ani mamaʃ mitsta'er.
אני ממש מצטער.

I'm really sorry. (woman ⇨)
ani mamaʃ mitsta"eret.
אני ממש מצטערת.

Sorry, it's my fault.
sliχa, zo aʃmati.
סליחה, זו אשמתי.

My mistake.
ta'ut ʃeli.
טעות שלי.

May I ...? (man ⇨)
ha'im ani yaχol ...?
האם אני יבול ...?

May I ...? (woman ⇨)
ha'im ani yeχola ...?
האם אני יבולה ...?

Do you mind if I ...? (⇨ man)
ha'im iχpat leχa im ani ...?
האם איכפת לך אם אני ...?

Do you mind if I ...? (⇨ woman)
ha'im iχpat laχ im ani ...?
האם איכפת לך אם אני ...?

It's OK.
ze be'seder.
זה בסדר.

It's all right.
ze be'seder.
זה בסדר.

Don't worry about it. (⇨ man)
al taχʃov al ze.
אל תחשוב על זה.

Don't worry about it. (⇨ woman)
al taχʃevi al ze.
אל תחשבי על זה.

Agreement

Yes.	ken.
	כן.
Yes, sure.	ken, bevadai.
	כן, בוודאי.
OK (Good!)	tov!
	טוב!
Very well.	be'seder gamur.
	בסדר גמור.
Certainly!	bevadai!
	בוודאי!
I agree. (man ⋄)	ani maskim.
	אני מסכים.
I agree. (woman ⋄)	ani maskima.
	אני מסכימה.
That's correct.	ze naxon.
	זה נכון.
That's right.	ze naxon.
	זה נכון.
You're right. (⋄ man)	ata tsodek.
	אתה צודק.
You're right. (⋄ woman)	at tso'deket.
	את צודקת.
I don't mind.	lo mefane li.
	לא משנה לי.
Absolutely right.	naxon me'od.
	נכון מאוד.
It's possible.	yitaxen, ze effari.
	ייתכן, זה אפשרי.
That's a good idea.	ze ra'ayon tov.
	זה רעיון טוב.
I can't say no. (man ⋄)	ani lo yaxol lesarev.
	אני לא יכול לסרב.
I can't say no. (woman ⋄)	ani lo yexola lesarev.
	אני לא יכולה לסרב.
I'd be happy to.	esmax la'asot et ze.
	אשמח לעשות את זה.
With pleasure.	bekef.
	בכיף.

Refusal. Expressing doubt

No.	lo. לא.
Certainly not.	ba'tuax ʃelo. בטוח שלא.
I don't agree. (man ⌐)	ani lo maskim. אני לא מסכים.
I don't agree. (woman ⌐)	ani lo maskima. אני לא מסכימה.
I don't think so. (man ⌐)	ani lo xoʃev kax. אני לא חושב כך.
I don't think so. (woman ⌐)	ani lo xoʃevet kax. אני לא חושבת כך.
It's not true.	ze lo naxon. זה לא נכון.
You are wrong. (⌐ man)	ata to'e. אתה טועה.
You are wrong. (⌐ woman)	at to'a. את טועה.
I think you are wrong. (man ⌐ man)	ani xoʃev ʃe'ata to'e. אני חושב שאתה טועה.
I think you are wrong. (man ⌐ woman)	ani xoʃev ʃe'at to'a. אני חושב שאת טועה.
I think you are wrong. (woman ⌐ man)	ani xo'ʃevet ʃe'ata to'e. אני חושבת שאתה טועה.
I think you are wrong. (woman ⌐ woman)	ani xo'ʃevet ʃe'at to'a. אני חושבת שאת טועה.
I'm not sure. (man ⌐)	ani lo ba'tuax. אני לא בטוח.
I'm not sure. (woman ⌐)	ani lo betuxa. אני לא בטוחה.
It's impossible.	ze 'bilti efʃari. זה בלתי אפשרי.
Nothing of the kind (sort)!	beʃum panim va''ofen lo! בשום פנים ואופן לא!
The exact opposite.	bediyuk ha'hefex. בדיוק ההיפך.
I'm against it. (man ⌐)	ani mitnaged leze. אני מתנגד לזה.
I'm against it. (woman ⌐)	ani mitna'gedet leze. אני מתנגדת לזה.
I don't care.	lo ixpat li. לא איכפת לי.

I have no idea.	ein li musag. אין לי מושג.
I doubt it. (man ☞)	ani lo ba'tuax. אני לא בטוח.
I doubt it. (woman ☞)	ani lo betuxa. אני לא בטוחה.

Sorry, I can't. (man ☞)	mitsta'er, ani lo yaxol. מצטער, אני לא יכול.
Sorry, I can't. (woman ☞)	mitsta"eret, ani lo yexola. מצטערת, אני לא יכולה.
Sorry, I don't want to. (man ☞)	mitsta'er, ani lo me'unyan. מצטער, אני לא מעוניין.
Sorry, I don't want to. (woman ☞)	mitsta"eret, ani lo me'un'yenet. מצטערת, אני לא מעוניינת.
Thank you, but I don't need this. (man ☞)	toda, aval ani lo tsarix et ze. תודה, אבל אני לא צריך את זה.
Thank you, but I don't need this. (woman ☞)	toda, aval ani lo tsrixa et ze. תודה, אבל אני לא צריכה את זה.

It's getting late.	matxil lihyot me'uxar. מתחיל להיות מאוחר.
I have to get up early. (man ☞)	ani tsarix lakum mukdam. אני צריך לקום מוקדם.
I have to get up early. (woman ☞)	ani tsrixa lakum mukdam. אני צריכה לקום מוקדם.
I don't feel well. (man ☞)	ani lo margiʃ tov. אני לא מרגיש טוב.
I don't feel well. (woman ☞)	ani lo margiʃa tov. אני לא מרגישה טוב.

Expressing gratitude

Thank you.	toda.
	תודה.
Thank you very much.	toda raba.
	תודה רבה.
I really appreciate it. (man ⇨)	ani be'emet ma'ariχ et ze.
	אני באמת מעריך את זה.
I really appreciate it. (woman ⇨)	ani be'emet ma'ariχa et ze.
	אני באמת מעריכה את זה.
I'm really grateful to you. (man ⇨ man)	ani mamaʃ asir toda leχa.
	אני ממש אסיר תודה לך.
I'm really grateful to you. (man ⇨ woman)	ani mamaʃ asir toda laχ.
	אני ממש אסיר תודה לך.
I'm really grateful to you. (woman ⇨ man)	ani mamaʃ asirat toda leχa.
	אני ממש אסירת תודה לך.
I'm really grateful to you. (woman ⇨ woman)	ani mamaʃ asirat toda laχ.
	אני ממש אסירת תודה לך.
Thank you for your time. (⇨ man)	toda al hazman ʃehik'daʃta.
	תודה על הזמן שהקדשת.
Thank you for your time. (⇨ woman)	toda al hazman ʃehikdaʃt.
	תודה על הזמן שהקדשת.
Thanks for everything.	toda al hakol.
	תודה על הכל.
Thank you for ...	toda al ...
	תודה על ...
your help (⇨ man)	ezratχa
	עזרתך
your help (⇨ woman)	ezrateχ
	עזרתך
a nice time	haχavaya hamehana
	החוויה המהנה
a wonderful meal	aruχa nehe'deret
	ארוחה נהדרת
a pleasant evening	erev na'im
	ערב נעים
a wonderful day	yom nifla
	יום נפלא
an amazing journey	tiyul madhim
	טיול מדהים
Don't mention it.	ein be'ad ma.
	אין בעד מה.
You are welcome.	bevakaʃa.
	בבקשה.

Any time.	ein be'ad ma. אין בעד מה.
My pleasure.	ha"oneg kulo ʃeli. העונג כולו שלי.
Forget it.	lo meʃane. לא משנה.
Don't worry about it. (⇨ man)	al tid'ag. אל תדאג.
Don't worry about it. (⇨ woman)	al tid'agi. אל תדאגי.

Congratulations. Best wishes

Congratulations!

birχotai!
ברכותיי!

Happy birthday!

mazal tov leyom hahu'ledet!
מזל טוב ליום ההולדת!

Merry Christmas!

χag molad sa'meaχ!
חג מולד שמח!

Happy New Year!

ʃana tova!
שנה טובה!

Happy Easter!

χag pasχa sa'meaχ!
חג פסחא שמח!

Happy Hanukkah!

χag 'χanuka sa'meaχ!
חג חנוכה שמח!

I'd like to propose a toast. (man ⇨)

ani rotse leharim kosit.
אני רוצה להרים כוסית.

I'd like to propose a toast. (woman ⇨)

ani rotsa leharim kosit.
אני רוצה להרים כוסית.

Cheers!

le'χayim!
לחיים!

Let's drink to …!

bo'u niʃte le …!
בואו נשתה ל ...!

To our success!

lehatslaχa'tenu!
להצלחתנו!

To your success! (⇨ man)

lehatslaχatχa!
להצלחתך!

To your success! (⇨ woman)

lehatslaχateχ!
להצלחתך!

Good luck!

behatslaχa!
בהצלחה!

Have a nice day! (⇨ man)

ʃeyihye leχa yom na'im!
שיהיה לך יום נעים!

Have a nice day! (⇨ woman)

ʃeyihye laχ yom na'im!
שיהיה לך יום נעים!

Have a good holiday!

χufʃa ne'ima!
חופשה נעימה!

Have a safe journey!

nesi'a tova!
נסיעה טובה!

I hope you get better soon!
(man ⇨ man)

ani mekave ʃetaχlim maher!
אני מקווה שתחלים מהר!

I hope you get better soon!
(man ⇨ woman)

ani mekave ʃetaχ'limi maher!
אני מקווה שתחלימי מהר!

I hope you get better soon!
(woman ⇔ man)

ani mekava ʃetaχlim maher!
אני מקווה שתחלים מהר!

I hope you get better soon!
(woman ⇔ woman)

ani mekava ʃetaχ'limi maher!
אני מקווה שתחלימי מהר!

Socializing

Why are you sad? (⇨ man)	lama ata atsuv? למה אתה עצוב?
Why are you sad? (⇨ woman)	lama at atsuva? למה את עצובה?
Smile! Cheer up! (⇨ man)	xayex ktsat! חייך קצת!
Smile! Cheer up! (⇨ woman)	xaixi ktsat! חייכי קצת!
Are you free tonight? (⇨ man)	ha'im ata panui ha''erev? האם אתה פנוי הערב?
Are you free tonight? (⇨ woman)	ha'im at pnuya ha''erev? האם את פנויה הערב?
May I offer you a drink?	ha'im efʃar leha'tsi'a lax maʃke? האם אפשר להציע לך משקה?
Would you like to dance? (⇨ man)	ha'im ata rotse lirkod? האם אתה רוצה לרקוד?
Would you like to dance? (⇨ woman)	ha'im at rotsa lirkod? האם את רוצה לרקוד?
Let's go to the movies. (⇨ man)	bo nelex le'seret. בוא נלך לסרט.
Let's go to the movies. (⇨ woman)	bo'i nelex le'seret. בואי נלך לסרט.
May I invite you to …?	ha'im efʃar lehazmin otax le …? האם אפשר להזמין אותך ל ...?
a restaurant	mis'ada מסעדה
the movies	seret סרט
the theater	te'atron תיאטרון
go for a walk	letiyul ba'regel לטיול ברגל
At what time?	be''eizo ʃa'a? באיזו שעה?
tonight	ha'laila הלילה
at six	beʃeʃ בשש
at seven	be'ʃeva בשבע

at eight	bi'ʃmone
	בשמונה
at nine	be'teʃa
	בתשע

Do you like it here? (⇨ man)	ha'im hamakom motse χen be'ei'neχa?
	?האם המקום מוצא חן בעיניך
Do you like it here? (⇨ woman)	ha'im hamakom motse χen be'ei'nayiχ?
	?האם המקום מוצא חן בעינייך
Are you here with someone? (⇨ man)	ha'im ata nimtsa kan im 'miʃehu?
	?האם אתה נמצא כאן עם מישהו
Are you here with someone? (⇨ woman)	ha'im at nimtset kan im 'miʃehu?
	?האם את נמצאת כאן עם מישהו
I'm with my friend.	ani kan im χaver /χavera/.
	.אני כאן עם חבר /חברה/
I'm with my friends.	ani kan im χaverim.
	.אני כאן עם חברים
No, I'm alone.	lo, ani levad.
	.לא, אני לבד
Do you have a boyfriend?	ha'im yeʃ laχ χaver?
	?האם יש לך חבר
I have a boyfriend.	yeʃ li χaver.
	.יש לי חבר
Do you have a girlfriend?	ha'im yeʃ leχa χavera?
	?האם יש לך חברה
I have a girlfriend.	yeʃ li χavera.
	.יש לי חברה

Can I see you again? (⇨ man)	ha'im tirtse lehipageʃ ʃuv?
	?האם תרצה להיפגש שוב
Can I see you again? (⇨ woman)	ha'im tirtsi lehipageʃ ʃuv?
	?האם תרצי להיפגש שוב
Can I call you? (man ⇨ man)	ha'im ani yaχol lehitkaʃer e'leχa?
	?האם אני יכול להתקשר אליך
Can I call you? (man ⇨ woman)	ha'im ani yaχol lehitkaʃer e'layiχ?
	?האם אני יכול להתקשר אלייך
Can I call you? (woman ⇨ man)	ha'im ani yeχola lehitkaʃer e'leχa?
	?האם אני יכולה להתקשר אליך
Can I call you? (woman ⇨ woman)	ha'im ani yeχola lehitkaʃer e'layiχ?
	?האם אני יכולה להתקשר אלייך
Call me. (Give me a call.) (⇨ man)	hitkaʃer elai.
	.התקשר אליי
Call me. (Give me a call.) (⇨ woman)	hitkaʃri elai.
	.התקשרי אליי
What's your number? (⇨ man)	ma hamispar ʃelχa?
	?מה המספר שלך
What's your number? (⇨ woman)	ma hamispar ʃelaχ?
	?מה המספר שלך
I miss you. (man ⇨ man)	ani mitga'a''ge'a e'leχa.
	.אני מתגעגע אליך
I miss you. (man ⇨ woman)	ani mitga'a''ge'a e'layiχ.
	.אני מתגעגע אלייך

I miss you. (woman ⇨ man)	ani mitga'a''ga'at e'leχa. אני מתגעגעת אליך.
I miss you. (woman ⇨ woman)	ani mitga'a''ga'at e'layiχ. אני מתגעגעת אלייך.
You have a beautiful name. (man ⇨ man)	yeʃ leχa ʃem maksim. יש לך שם מקסים.
You have a beautiful name. (man ⇨ woman)	yeʃ laχ ʃem maksim. יש לך שם מקסים.
I love you.	ani ohev otaχ. אני אוהב אותך.
Will you marry me?	ha'im titχatni iti? האם תתחתני איתי?
You're kidding!	at tso'χeket alai! את צוחקת עליי!
I'm just kidding. (man ⇨)	ani stam mitba'deaχ. אני סתם מתבדח.
I'm just kidding. (woman ⇨)	ani stam mitba'daχat. אני סתם מתבדחת.
Are you serious? (⇨ man)	ha'im ata retsini? האם אתה רציני?
Are you serious? (⇨ woman)	ha'im at retsinit? האם את רצינית?
I'm serious. (man ⇨)	ani retsini. אני רציני.
I'm serious. (woman ⇨)	ani retsinit. אני רצינית.
Really?!	be'emet?! באמת?!
It's unbelievable!	ze lo ye'uman! זה לא יאומן!
I don't believe you. (man ⇨ man)	ani lo ma'amin leχa. אני לא מאמין לך.
I don't believe you. (man ⇨ woman)	ani lo ma'amin laχ. אני לא מאמין לך.
I don't believe you. (woman ⇨ man)	ani lo ma'amina leχa. אני לא מאמינה לך.
I don't believe you. (woman ⇨ woman)	ani lo ma'amina laχ. אני לא מאמינה לך.
I can't. (man ⇨)	ani lo yaχol. אני לא יכול.
I can't. (woman ⇨)	ani lo yeχola. אני לא יכולה.
I don't know. (man ⇨)	ani lo yo'de'a. אני לא יודע.
I don't know. (woman ⇨)	ani lo yo'da'at. אני לא יודעת.
I don't understand you. (man ⇨ man)	ani lo mevin otχa. אני לא מבין אותך.

I don't understand you. (man ⇨ woman)	ani lo mevin otaχ
	אני לא מבין אותך.
I don't understand you. (woman ⇨ man)	ani lo mevina otχa.
	אני לא מבינה אותך.
I don't understand you. (woman ⇨ woman)	ani lo mevina otaχ.
	אני לא מבינה אותך.
Please go away. (⇨ man)	leχ mipo bevakaʃa.
	לך מפה בבקשה.
Please go away. (⇨ woman)	leχi mipo bevakaʃa.
	לכי מפה בבקשה.
Leave me alone! (⇨ man)	azov oti!
	עזוב אותי!
Leave me alone! (⇨ woman)	izvi oti!
	עזבי אותי!

I can't stand him. (man ⇨)	ani lo sovel oto.
	אני לא סובל אותו.
I can't stand him. (woman ⇨)	ani lo so'velet oto.
	אני לא סובלת אותו.
You are disgusting! (⇨ man)	ata mag'il!
	אתה מגעיל!
You are disgusting! (⇨ woman)	at mag'ila!
	את מגעילה!
I'll call the police!	ani azmin miʃtara!
	אני אזמין משטרה!

Sharing impressions. Emotions

I like it.	ze motse χen be'einai. זה מוצא חן בעיניי.
Very nice.	neχmad me'od. נחמד מאוד.
That's great!	ze nehedar! זה נהדר!
It's not bad.	ze lo ra. זה לא רע.

I don't like it.	ze lo motse χen be'einai. זה לא מוצא חן בעיניי.
It's not good.	ze lo yafe. זה לא יפה.
It's bad.	ze ra. זה רע.
It's very bad.	ze ra me'od. זה רע מאוד.
It's disgusting.	ze mag'il. זה מגעיל.

I'm happy. (man ☺)	ani me'uʃar. אני מאושר.
I'm happy. (woman ☺)	ani me'uʃeret. אני מאושרת.
I'm content. (man ☺)	ani merutse. אני מרוצה.
I'm content. (woman ☺)	ani merutsa. אני מרוצה.
I'm in love. (man ☺)	ani me'ohav. אני מאוהב.
I'm in love. (woman ☺)	ani me'o'hevet. אני מאוהבת.
I'm calm. (man ☺)	ani ra'gu'a. אני רגוע.
I'm calm. (woman ☺)	ani regu'a. אני רגועה.
I'm bored. (man ☺)	ani meʃu'amam. אני משועמם.
I'm bored. (woman ☺)	ani meʃu'a'memet. אני משועממת.
I'm tired. (man ☺)	ani ayef. אני עייף.
I'm tired. (woman ☺)	ani ayefa. אני עייפה.

I'm sad. (man ☞)	ani atsuv.
	אני עצוב.
I'm sad. (woman ☞)	ani atsuva.
	אני עצובה.
I'm frightened. (man ☞)	ani poxed.
	אני פוחד.
I'm frightened. (woman ☞)	ani po'xedet.
	אני פוחדת.
I'm angry. (man ☞)	ani ko'es.
	אני כועס.
I'm angry. (woman ☞)	ani ko''eset.
	אני כועסת.
I'm worried. (man ☞)	ani mud'ag.
	אני מודאג.
I'm worried. (woman ☞)	ani mud''eget.
	אני מודאגת.
I'm nervous. (man ☞)	ani atsbani.
	אני עצבני.
I'm nervous. (woman ☞)	ani atsbanit.
	אני עצבנית.
I'm jealous. (envious) (man ☞)	ani mekane.
	אני מקנא.
I'm jealous. (envious) (woman ☞)	ani mekanet.
	אני מקנאת.
I'm surprised. (man ☞)	ani mufta.
	אני מופתע.
I'm surprised. (woman ☞)	ani mufta'at.
	אני מופתעת.
I'm perplexed. (man ☞)	ani mevulbal.
	אני מבולבל.
I'm perplexed. (woman ☞)	ani mevul'belet.
	אני מבולבלת.

Problems. Accidents

I've got a problem.	yeʃ li be'aya. יש לי בעייה.
We've got a problem.	yeʃ 'lanu be'aya. יש לנו בעייה.
I'm lost.	ha'laχti le'ibud. הלכתי לאיבוד.
I missed the last bus.	fis'fasti et ha''otobus ha'aχaron. פספסתי את האוטובוס האחרון.
I missed the last train.	fis'fasti et hara'kevet ha'aχrona. פספסתי את הרכבת האחרונה.
I don't have any money left.	niʃ'arti bli 'kesef. נשארתי בלי כסף.

I've lost my ...	i'badti et ha... ʃeli איבדתי את ה... שלי
Someone stole my ...	miʃehu ganav et ha... ʃeli מישהו גנב את ה... שלי
passport	darkon דרכון
wallet	arnak ארנק
papers	te'udot תעודות
ticket	kartis כרטיס

money	kesef כסף
handbag	tik yad תיק יד
camera	matslema מצלמה
laptop	maχʃev nayad מחשב נייד
tablet computer	maχʃev ʃulχani מחשב שולחני
mobile phone	telefon nayad טלפון נייד

Help me!	izru li! עזרו לי!
What's happened?	ma kara? מה קרה?

fire	srefa שריפה
shooting	yeriyot יריות
murder	retsaχ רצח
explosion	pitsuts פיצוץ
fight	ktata קטטה

Call the police!	haz'minu miʃtara הזמינו משטרה!
Please hurry up!	ana maharu! אנא מהרו!
I'm looking for the police station. (man ⇨)	ani meχapes et taχanat hamiʃtara. אני מחפש את תחנת המשטרה.
I'm looking for the police station. (woman ⇨)	ani meχa'peset et taχanat hamiʃtara. אני מחפשת את תחנת המשטרה.
I need to make a call. (man ⇨)	ani tsariχ lehitkaʃer. אני צריך להתקשר.
I need to make a call. (woman ⇨)	ani tsriχa lehitkaʃer. אני צריכה להתקשר.
May I use your phone? (⇨ man)	ha'im efʃar lehiʃtameʃ be'telefon ʃelχa? האם אפשר להשתמש בטלפון שלך?
May I use your phone? (⇨ woman)	ha'im efʃar lehiʃtameʃ be'telefon ʃelaχ? האם אפשר להשתמש בטלפון שלך?

I've been …	ani … אני ...
mugged	hut'kafti הותקפתי
robbed	niʃ'dadti נשדדתי
raped	ne'e'nasti נאנסתי
attacked (beaten up)	hu'keti הוכיתי

Are you all right? (⇨ man)	ha'im ata be'seder? האם אתה בסדר?
Are you all right? (⇨ woman)	ha'im at be'seder? האם את בסדר?
Did you see who it was? (⇨ man)	ha'im ra''ita mi asa et ze? האם ראית מי עשה את זה?
Did you see who it was? (⇨ woman)	ha'im ra'it mi asa et ze? האם ראית מי עשה את זה?
Would you be able to recognize the person? (⇨ man)	ha'im tuχal lezahot et oto adam? האם תוכל לזהות את אותו אדם?
Would you be able to recognize the person? (⇨ woman)	ha'im tuχli lezahot et oto adam? האם תוכלי לזהות את אותו אדם?

Are you sure? (⇨ man)	ha'im ata ba'tuax? האם אתה בטוח?
Are you sure? (⇨ woman)	ha'im at betuxa? האם את בטוחה?

Please calm down. (⇨ man)	heraga, bevakaʃa. הירגע בבקשה.
Please calm down. (⇨ woman)	herag'i, bevakaʃa. הירגעי בבקשה.
Take it easy! (⇨ man)	teraga! תירגע!
Take it easy! (⇨ woman)	terag'i! תירגעי!
Don't worry! (⇨ man)	al tid'ag! אל תדאג!
Don't worry! (⇨ woman)	al tid'agi! אל תדאגי!
Everything will be fine.	hakol yihye be'seder. הכל יהיה בסדר.
Everything's all right.	hakol be'seder. הכל בסדר.

Come here, please. (⇨ man)	bo 'hena, bevakaʃa. בוא הנה, בבקשה.
Come here, please. (⇨ woman)	bo'i 'hena, bevakaʃa. בואי הנה, בבקשה.
I have some questions for you. (⇨ man)	yeʃ li 'kama ʃe'elot e'lexa. יש לי כמה שאלות אליך.
I have some questions for you. (⇨ woman)	yeʃ li 'kama ʃe'elot e'layix. יש לי כמה שאלות אלייך.
Wait a moment, please. (⇨ man)	xake 'rega, bevakaʃa. חכה רגע, בבקשה.
Wait a moment, please. (⇨ woman)	xaki 'rega, bevakaʃa. חכי רגע, בבקשה.
Do you have any I.D.? (⇨ man)	ha'im yeʃ lexa te'uda mezaha? האם יש לך תעודה מזהה?
Do you have any I.D.? (⇨ woman)	ha'im yeʃ lax te'uda mezaha? האם יש לך תעודה מזהה?
Thanks. You can leave now. (⇨ man)	toda. ata yaxol la'lexet axʃav. תודה. אתה יכול ללכת עכשיו.
Thanks. You can leave now. (⇨ woman)	toda. at yexola la'lexet axʃav. תודה. את יכולה ללכת עכשיו.
Hands behind your head!	ya'dayim axarei haroʃ! ידיים אחרי הראש!
You're under arrest! (⇨ man)	ata atsur! אתה עצור!
You're under arrest! (⇨ woman)	at atsura! את עצורה!

Health problems

Please help me. (⇨ man)	azor li bevakaʃa. עזור לי בבקשה.
Please help me. (⇨ woman)	izri li bevakaʃa. עזרי לי בבקשה.
I don't feel well. (man ⇨)	ani lo margiʃ tov. אני לא מרגיש טוב.
I don't feel well. (woman ⇨)	ani lo margiʃa tov. אני לא מרגישה טוב.
My husband doesn't feel well.	ba'ali lo margiʃ tov. בעלי לא מרגיש טוב.
My son …	haben ʃeli … הבן שלי …
My father …	avi … אבי …
My wife doesn't feel well.	iʃti lo margiʃa tov. אשתי לא מרגישה טוב.
My daughter …	habat ʃeli … הבת שלי …
My mother …	immi … אמי …
I've got a …	yeʃ li … יש לי …
headache	ke'ev roʃ כאב ראש
sore throat	ke'ev garon כאב גרון
stomach ache	ke'ev 'beten כאב בטן
toothache	ke'ev ʃi'nayim כאב שיניים
I feel dizzy.	yeʃ li sxar'xoret. יש לי סחרחורת.
He has a fever.	yeʃ lo xom. יש לו חום.
She has a fever.	yeʃ la xom. יש לה חום.
I can't breathe. (man ⇨)	ani lo yaxol linʃom. אני לא יכול לנשום.
I can't breathe. (woman ⇨)	ani lo yexola linʃom. אני לא יכולה לנשום.

I'm short of breath.

ye∫ li 'kotser ne∫ima.
יש לי קוצר נשימה.

I am asthmatic. (man ⇨)

ani ast'mati.
אני אסתמתי.

I am asthmatic. (woman ⇨)

ani ast'matit.
אני אסתמתית.

I am diabetic.

ye∫ li su'keret.
יש לי סוכרת.

I can't sleep. (man ⇨)

ani lo yaxol li∫on.
אני לא יכול לישון.

I can't sleep. (woman ⇨)

ani lo yexola li∫on.
אני לא יכולה לישון.

food poisoning

har'alat mazon
הרעלת מזון

It hurts here.

ko'ev li kan.
כואב לי כאן.

Help me!

izru li!
עזרו לי!

I am here!

ani po!
אני פה!

We are here!

a'naxnu kan!
אנחנו כאן!

Get me out of here!

hots'i'u oti mikan!
הוציאו אותי מכאן!

I need a doctor. (man ⇨)

ani tsarix rofe.
אני צריך רופא.

I need a doctor. (woman ⇨)

ani tsrixa rofe.
אני צריכה רופא.

I can't move. (man ⇨)

ani lo yaxol lazuz.
אני לא יכול לזוז.

I can't move. (woman ⇨)

ani lo yexola lazuz.
אני לא יכולה לזוז.

I can't move my legs. (man ⇨)

ani lo yaxol lehaziz et harag'layim.
אני לא יכול להזיז את הרגליים.

I can't move my legs. (woman ⇨)

ani lo yexola lehaziz et harag'layim.
אני לא יכולה להזיז את הרגליים.

I have a wound.

ye∫ li 'petsa.
יש לי פצע.

Is it serious?

ha'im ze retsini?
האם זה רציני?

My documents are in my pocket.

hate'udot ∫eli bakis.
התעודות שלי בכיס.

Calm down! (⇨ man)

heraga!
הירגע!

Calm down! (⇨ woman)

herag'i!
הירגעי!

May I use your phone? (man ⇨ man)

ha'im ani yaxol lehi∫tame∫
ba'telefon ∫elxa?
האם אני יכול להשתמש
בטלפון שלך?

May I use your phone? (man ⇨ woman)	ha'im ani yaχol lehiʃtameʃ ba'telefon ʃelaχ? האם אני יכול להשתמש בטלפון שלך?
May I use your phone? (woman ⇨ woman)	ha'im ani yeχola lehiʃtameʃ ba'telefon ʃelaχ? האם אני יכולה להשתמש בטלפון שלך?
May I use your phone? (woman ⇨ man)	ha'im ani yeχola lehiʃtameʃ ba'telefon ʃelχa? האם אני יכולה להשתמש בטלפון שלך?

Call an ambulance!	haz'minu 'ambulans! הזמינו אמבולנס!
It's urgent!	ze daχuf! זה דחוף!
It's an emergency!	ze matsav χerum! זה מצב חירום!
Please hurry up!	ana maharu! אנא מהרו!
Would you please call a doctor? (⇨ man)	ha'im ata yaχol lehazmin rofe, bevakaʃa? האם אתה יכול להזמין רופא בבקשה?
Would you please call a doctor? (⇨ woman)	ha'im at yeχola lehazmin rofe, bevakaʃa? האם את יכולה להזמין רופא בבקשה?
Where is the hospital?	eifo beit haχolim? איפה בית החולים?

How are you feeling? (⇨ man)	eiχ ata margiʃ? איך אתה מרגיש?
How are you feeling? (⇨ woman)	eiχ at margiʃa? איך את מרגישה?
Are you all right? (⇨ man)	ha'im ata be'seder? האם אתה בסדר?
Are you all right? (⇨ woman)	ha'im at be'seder? האם את בסדר?
What's happened?	ma kara? מה קרה?
I feel better now. (man ⇨)	ani margiʃ yoter tov aχʃav. אני מרגיש טוב יותר עכשיו.
I feel better now. (woman ⇨)	ani margiʃa yoter tov aχʃav. אני מרגישה טוב יותר עכשיו.
It's OK.	ze be'seder. זה בסדר.
It's all right.	ze be'seder. זה בסדר.

At the pharmacy

pharmacy (drugstore)	beit mer'kaxat בית מרקחת
24-hour pharmacy	beit mer'kaxat pa'tuax esrim ve'arba ʃa'ot biymama בית מרקחת פתוח עשרים וארבע שעות ביממה
Where is the closest pharmacy?	eifo beit hamer'kaxat hakarov beyoter? איפה בית המרקחת הקרוב ביותר?

Is it open now?	ha'im ze pa'tuax axʃav? האם זה פתוח עכשיו?
At what time does it open?	be''eizo ʃa'a ze niftax? באיזו שעה זה נפתח?
At what time does it close?	be''eizo ʃa'a ze nisgar? באיזו שעה זה נסגר?

Is it far?	ha'im ze raxok? האם זה רחוק?
Can I get there on foot? (man ⇨)	ha'im ani yaxol la'lexet leʃam ba'regel? האם אני יכול ללכת לשם ברגל?
Can I get there on foot? (woman ⇨)	ha'im ani yexola la'lexet leʃam ba'regel? האם אני יכולה ללכת לשם ברגל?
Can you show me on the map? (⇨ man)	ha'im ata yaxol lehar'ot li al hamapa? האם אתה יכול להראות לי על המפה?
Can you show me on the map? (⇨ woman)	ha'im at yexola lehar'ot li al hamapa? האם את יכולה להראות לי על המפה?

Please give me something for … (⇨ man)	ten li bevakaʃa 'maʃehu 'neged … תן לי בבקשה משהו נגד ...
Please give me something for … (⇨ woman)	tni li bevakaʃa 'maʃehu 'neged … תני לי בבקשה משהו נגד ...
a headache	ke'ev roʃ כאב ראש
a cough	ʃi'ul שיעול
a cold	hitkarerut התקררות
the flu	ʃa'pa'at שפעת

a fever	xom חום
a stomach ache	ke'ev 'beten כאב בטן

nausea	bχila
	בחילה
diarrhea	ſilſul
	שלשול
constipation	atsirut
	עצירות

pain in the back	ke'ev bagav
	כאב בגב
chest pain	ke'ev baχaze
	כאב בחזה
side stitch	dkirot batsad
	דקירות בצד
abdominal pain	ke'ev ba'beten
	כאב בבטן

pill	glula
	גלולה
ointment, cream	miſχa, krem
	משחה, קרם
syrup	sirop
	סירופ
spray	tarsis
	תרסיס
drops	tipot
	טיפות

You need to go to the hospital. (⇨ man)	ata tsariχ la'leχet leveit χolim.
	אתה צריך ללכת לבית חולים.
You need to go to the hospital. (⇨ woman)	at tsriχa la'leχet leveit χolim.
	את צריכה ללכת לבית חולים.
health insurance	bi'tuaχ bri'ut
	ביטוח בריאות
prescription	mirſam
	מרשם
insect repellant	doχe χarakim
	דוחה חרקים
Band Aid	plaster
	פלסטר

The bare minimum

Excuse me, ... (⇨ man)	slaχ li, ... סלח לי, ...
Excuse me, ... (⇨ woman)	silχi li, ... סלחי לי, ...
Hello.	ʃalom. שלום.
Thank you.	toda. תודה.
Good bye.	lehitra'ot. להתראות.
Yes.	ken. כן.
No.	lo. לא.
I don't know. (man ⇨)	ani lo yo'de'a. אני לא יודע.
I don't know. (woman ⇨)	ani lo yo'da'at. אני לא יודעת.
Where?	Where to?	When?	eifo?	le'an?	matai? איפה?	לאן?	מתי?
I need ... (man ⇨)	ani tsariχ ... אני צריך ...
I need ... (woman ⇨)	ani tsriχa ... אני צריכה ...
I want ... (man ⇨)	ani rotse ... אני רוצה ...
I want ... (woman ⇨)	ani rotsa ... אני רוצה ...
Do you have ...? (⇨ man)	ha'im yeʃ leχa ...? האם יש לך ...?
Do you have ...? (⇨ woman)	ha'im yeʃ laχ ...? האם יש לך ...?
Is there a ... here?	ha'im yeʃ po ...? האם יש פה ...?
May I ...? (man ⇨)	ha'im ani yaχol ...? האם אני יכול ...?
May I ...? (woman ⇨)	ha'im ani yeχola ...? האם אני יכולה ...?
..., please (polite request)	..., bevakaʃa ..., בבקשה

I'm looking for ... (man ⇨)	ani meχapes ... אני מחפש ...
I'm looking for ... (woman ⇨)	ani meχa'peset ... אני מחפשת ...
the restroom	ʃerutim שירותים
an ATM	kaspomat כספומט
a pharmacy (drugstore)	beit mer'kaχat בית מרקחת
a hospital	beit χolim בית חולים
the police station	taχanat miʃtara תחנת משטרה
the subway	ra'kevet taχtit רכבת תחתית
a taxi	monit, 'teksi מונית, טקסי
the train station	taχanat ra'kevet תחנת רכבת

My name is ...	kor'im li ... קוראים לי ...
What's your name? (⇨ man)	eiχ kor'im leχa? איך קוראים לך?
What's your name? (⇨ woman)	eiχ kor'im laχ? איך קוראים לך?
Could you please help me? (⇨ man)	ha'im ata yaχol la'azor li? האם אתה יכול לעזור לי?
Could you please help me? (⇨ woman)	ha'im at yeχola la'azor li? האם את יכולה לעזור לי?
I've got a problem.	yeʃ li be'aya. יש לי בעייה.
I don't feel well. (man ⇨)	ani lo margiʃ tov. אני לא מרגיש טוב.
I don't feel well. (woman ⇨)	ani lo margiʃa tov. אני לא מרגישה טוב.
Call an ambulance! (⇨ man)	hazmen 'ambulans! הזמן אמבולנס!
Call an ambulance! (⇨ woman)	haz'mini 'ambulans! הזמיני אמבולנס!
May I make a call? (man ⇨)	ha'im ani yaχol lehitkaʃer? האם אני יכול להתקשר?
May I make a call? (woman ⇨)	ha'im ani yeχola lehitkaʃer? האם אני יכולה להתקשר?

I'm sorry. (man ⇨)	ani mitsta'er. אני מצטער.
I'm sorry. (woman ⇨)	ani mitsta"eret. אני מצטערת.
You're welcome.	ein be'ad ma, bevakaʃa. אין בעד מה, בבקשה.

I, me	ani
	אני
you (inform.) (masc.)	ata
	אתה
you (inform.) (fem.)	at
	את
he	hu
	הוא
she	hi
	היא
they (masc.)	hem
	הם
they (fem.)	hen
	הן
we	a'naχnu
	אנחנו
you (pl) (masc.)	atem
	אתם
you (pl) (fem.)	aten
	אתן
you (sg, form.) (masc.)	ata
	אתה
you (sg, form.) (fem.)	at
	את

ENTRANCE	knisa
	כניסה
EXIT	yetsi'a
	יציאה
OUT OF ORDER	lo po'el
	לא פועל
CLOSED	sagur
	סגור
OPEN	pa'tuaχ
	פתוח
FOR WOMEN	lenaʃim
	לנשים
FOR MEN	ligvarim
	לגברים

MINI DICTIONARY

This section contains 250
useful words required for
everyday communication.
You will find the names of
months and days of the week
here. The dictionary also
contains topics such as colors,
measurements, family, and
more

T&P Books Publishing

DICTIONARY CONTENTS

T&P Books Publishing

1. Time. Calendar

time	zman	זְמַן (ז)
hour	ʃa'a	שָׁעָה (נ)
half an hour	χatsi ʃa'a	חֲצִי שָׁעָה (נ)
minute	daka	דָּקָה (נ)
second	ʃniya	שְׁנִיָּה (נ)

today (adv)	hayom	הַיּוֹם
tomorrow (adv)	maχar	מָחָר
yesterday (adv)	etmol	אֶתְמוֹל

Monday	yom ʃeni	יוֹם שֵׁנִי (ז)
Tuesday	yom ʃliʃi	יוֹם שְׁלִישִׁי (ז)
Wednesday	yom revi'i	יוֹם רְבִיעִי (ז)
Thursday	yom χamiʃi	יוֹם חֲמִישִׁי (ז)
Friday	yom ʃiʃi	יוֹם שִׁישִׁי (ז)
Saturday	ʃabat	שַׁבָּת (נ)
Sunday	yom riʃon	יוֹם רִאשׁוֹן (ז)

day	yom	יוֹם (ז)
working day	yom avoda	יוֹם עֲבוֹדָה (ז)
public holiday	yom χag	יוֹם חַג (ז)
weekend	sof ʃa'vu'a	סוֹף שָׁבוּעַ

week	ʃa'vua	שָׁבוּעַ (ז)
last week (adv)	baʃa'vu'a ʃe'avar	בַּשָׁבוּעַ שֶׁעָבַר
next week (adv)	baʃa'vu'a haba	בַּשָׁבוּעַ הַבָּא

| in the morning | ba'boker | בַּבּוֹקֶר |
| in the afternoon | aχar hatsaha'rayim | אַחַר הַצָּהֳרַיִים |

| in the evening | ba''erev | בָּעֶרֶב |
| tonight (this evening) | ha''erev | הָעֶרֶב |

| at night | ba'laila | בַּלַּיְלָה |
| midnight | χatsot | חֲצוֹת (נ) |

January	'yanu'ar	יָנוּאָר (ז)
February	'febru'ar	פֶבְּרוּאָר (ז)
March	merts	מֶרְץ (ז)
April	april	אַפְּרִיל (ז)
May	mai	מַאי (ז)
June	'yuni	יוּנִי (ז)

| July | 'yuli | יוּלִי (ז) |
| August | 'ogust | אוֹגוּסְט (ז) |

September	sep'tember	סֶפְּטֶמְבֶּר (ז)
October	ok'tober	אוֹקְטוֹבֶּר (ז)
November	no'vember	נוֹבֶמְבֶּר (ז)
December	de'tsember	דֶּצֶמְבֶּר (ז)

in spring	ba'aviv	בָּאָבִיב
in summer	ba'kayits	בַּקַיִץ
in fall	bestav	בְּסְתָיו
in winter	ba'xoref	בַּחוֹרֶף

month	'xodeʃ	חוֹדֶש (ז)
season (summer, etc.)	ona	עוֹנָה (נ)
year	ʃana	שָׁנָה (נ)

2. Numbers. Numerals

0 zero	'efes	אֶפֶס (ז)
1 one	exad	אֶחָד (ז)
2 two	'ʃtayim	שְׁתַיִים (נ)
3 three	ʃaloʃ	שָׁלוֹש (נ)
4 four	arba	אַרְבַּע (נ)

5 five	xameʃ	חָמֵש (נ)
6 six	ʃeʃ	שֵׁש (נ)
7 seven	'ʃeva	שֶׁבַע (נ)
8 eight	'ʃmone	שְׁמוֹנֶה (נ)
9 nine	'teʃa	תֵּשַׁע (נ)
10 ten	'eser	עֶשֶׂר (נ)

11 eleven	axat esre	אַחַת־עֶשְׂרֵה (נ)
12 twelve	ʃteim esre	שְׁתֵּים־עֶשְׂרֵה (נ)
13 thirteen	ʃloʃ esre	שְׁלוֹש־עֶשְׂרֵה (נ)
14 fourteen	arba esre	אַרְבַּע־עֶשְׂרֵה (נ)
15 fifteen	xameʃ esre	חֲמֵש־עֶשְׂרֵה (נ)

16 sixteen	ʃeʃ esre	שֵׁש־עֶשְׂרֵה (נ)
17 seventeen	ʃva esre	שְׁבַע־עֶשְׂרֵה (נ)
18 eighteen	ʃmone esre	שְׁמוֹנֶה־עֶשְׂרֵה (נ)
19 nineteen	tʃa esre	תְּשַׁע־עֶשְׂרֵה (נ)

20 twenty	esrim	עֶשְׂרִים
30 thirty	ʃloʃim	שְׁלוֹשִׁים
40 forty	arba'im	אַרְבָּעִים
50 fifty	xamiʃim	חֲמִישִׁים

60 sixty	ʃiʃim	שִׁישִׁים
70 seventy	ʃiv'im	שִׁבְעִים
80 eighty	ʃmonim	שְׁמוֹנִים
90 ninety	tiʃ'im	תִּשְׁעִים
100 one hundred	'me'a	מֵאָה (נ)

200 two hundred	ma'tayim	מָאתַיִים
300 three hundred	ʃloʃ me'ot	שְׁלוֹשׁ מֵאוֹת (נ)
400 four hundred	arba me'ot	אַרְבַּע מֵאוֹת (נ)
500 five hundred	χameʃ me'ot	חָמֵשׁ מֵאוֹת (נ)
600 six hundred	ʃeʃ me'ot	שֵׁשׁ מֵאוֹת (נ)
700 seven hundred	ʃva me'ot	שְׁבַע מֵאוֹת (נ)
800 eight hundred	ʃmone me'ot	שְׁמוֹנֶה מֵאוֹת (נ)
900 nine hundred	tʃa me'ot	תֵּשַׁע מֵאוֹת (נ)
1000 one thousand	'elef	אֶלֶף (ז)
10000 ten thousand	a'seret alafim	עֲשֶׂרֶת אֲלָפִים (ז)
one hundred thousand	'me'a 'elef	מֵאָה אֶלֶף (ז)
million	milyon	מִילְיוֹן (ז)
billion	milyard	מִילְיַארְד (ז)

3. Humans. Family

man (adult male)	'gever	גֶּבֶר (ז)
young man	baχur	בָּחוּר (ז)
woman	iʃa	אִשָּׁה (נ)
girl (young woman)	baχura	בַּחוּרָה (נ)
old man	zaken	זָקֵן (ז)
old woman	zkena	זְקֵנָה (נ)
mother	em	אֵם (נ)
father	av	אָב (ז)
son	ben	בֵּן (ז)
daughter	bat	בַּת (נ)
brother	aχ	אָח (ז)
sister	aχot	אָחוֹת (נ)
parents	horim	הוֹרִים (ז״ר)
child	'yeled	יֶלֶד (ז)
children	yeladim	יְלָדִים (ז״ר)
stepmother	em χoreget	אֵם חוֹרֶגֶת (נ)
stepfather	av χoreg	אָב חוֹרֵג (ז)
grandmother	'savta	סָבְתָא (נ)
grandfather	'saba	סַבָּא (ז)
grandson	'neχed	נֶכֶד (ז)
granddaughter	neχda	נֶכְדָה (נ)
grandchildren	neχadim	נְכָדִים (ז״ר)
uncle	dod	דּוֹד (ז)
aunt	'doda	דּוֹדָה (נ)
nephew	aχyan	אַחְיָן (ז)
niece	aχyanit	אַחְיָינִית (נ)
wife	iʃa	אִשָּׁה (נ)

husband	'ba'al	בַּעַל (ז)
married (masc.)	nasui	נָשׂוּי
married (fem.)	nesu'a	נְשׂוּאָה
widow	almana	אַלְמָנָה (נ)
widower	alman	אַלְמָן (ז)

| name (first name) | ʃem | שֵׁם (ז) |
| surname (last name) | ʃem miʃpaχa | שֵׁם מִשְׁפָּחָה (ז) |

relative	karov miʃpaχa	קָרוֹב מִשְׁפָּחָה (ז)
friend (masc.)	χaver	חָבֵר (ז)
friendship	yedidut	יְדִידוּת (נ)

partner	ʃutaf	שׁוּתָף (ז)
superior (n)	memune	מְמוּנֶה (ז)
colleague	amit	עָמִית (ז)
neighbors	ʃχenim	שְׁכֵנִים (ז״ר)

4. Human body

body	guf	גוּף (ז)
heart	lev	לֵב (ז)
blood	dam	דָם (ז)
brain	'moaχ	מוֹחַ (ז)

bone	'etsem	עֶצֶם (נ)
spine (backbone)	amud haʃidra	עַמוּד הַשִׁדְרָה (ז)
rib	'tsela	צֶלַע (ז)
lungs	re'ot	רֵיאוֹת (נ״ר)
skin	or	עוֹר (ז)

head	roʃ	רֹאשׁ (ז)
face	panim	פָּנִים (ז״ר)
nose	af	אַף (ז)
forehead	'metsaχ	מֵצַח (ז)
cheek	'leχi	לֶחִי (נ)

mouth	pe	פֶּה (ז)
tongue	laʃon	לָשׁוֹן (נ)
tooth	ʃen	שֵׁן (נ)
lips	sfa'tayim	שְׂפָתַיִים (נ״ר)
chin	santer	סַנְטֵר (ז)

ear	'ozen	אוֹזֶן (נ)
neck	tsavar	צַוָּאר (ז)
eye	'ayin	עַיִן (נ)
pupil	iʃon	אִישׁוֹן (ז)
eyebrow	gaba	גַבָּה (נ)
eyelash	ris	רִיס (ז)
hair	se'ar	שֵׂיעָר (ז)

hairstyle	tis'roket	תִּסְרוֹקֶת (נ)
mustache	safam	שָׂפָם (ז)
beard	zakan	זָקָן (ז)
to have (a beard, etc.)	legadel	לְגַדֵל
bald (adj)	ke'reax	קֵירֵחַ

hand	kaf yad	כַּף יָד (נ)
arm	yad	יָד (נ)
finger	'etsba	אֶצְבַּע (נ)
nail	tsi'poren	צִיפּוֹרֶן (נ)
palm	kaf yad	כַּף יָד (נ)

shoulder	katef	כָּתֵף (נ)
leg	'regel	רֶגֶל (נ)
knee	'berex	בֶּרֶךְ (נ)
heel	akev	עָקֵב (ז)
back	gav	גַב (ז)

5. Clothing. Personal accessories

clothes	bgadim	בְּגָדִים (ז"ר)
coat (overcoat)	me'il	מְעִיל (ז)
fur coat	me'il parva	מְעִיל פַּרְוָה (ז)
jacket (e.g., leather ~)	me'il katsar	מְעִיל קָצָר (ז)
raincoat (trenchcoat, etc.)	me'il 'gefem	מְעִיל גֶשֶׁם (ז)

shirt (button shirt)	xultsa	חוּלְצָה (נ)
pants	mixna'sayim	מִכְנָסַיִים (ז"ר)
suit jacket	ʒaket	זָ'קֵט (ז)
suit	xalifa	חֲלִיפָה (נ)

dress (frock)	simla	שִׂמְלָה (נ)
skirt	xatsa'it	חֲצָאִית (נ)
T-shirt	ti ʃert	טִי שֶׁרְט (ז)
bathrobe	xaluk raxatsa	חָלוּק רַחְצָה (ז)
pajamas	pi'dʒama	פִּיגָ'מָה (נ)
workwear	bigdei avoda	בִּגְדֵי עֲבוֹדָה (ז"ר)

underwear	levanim	לְבָנִים (ז"ר)
socks	gar'bayim	גַרְבַּיִים (ז"ר)
bra	xaziya	חֲזִייָה (נ)
pantyhose	garbonim	גַרְבּוֹנִים (ז"ר)
stockings (thigh highs)	garbei 'nailon	גַרְבֵּי נַיְילוֹן (ז"ר)
bathing suit	'beged yam	בֶּגֶד יָם (ז)

hat	'kova	כּוֹבַע (ז)
footwear	han'ala	הַנְעָלָה (נ)
boots (e.g., cowboy ~)	maga'fayim	מַגָפַיִים (ז"ר)
heel	akev	עָקֵב (ז)
shoestring	srox	שְׂרוֹךְ (ז)

shoe polish	miʃχat na'a'layim	מִשְׁחַת נַעֲלַיִים (נ)
gloves	kfafot	כְּפָפוֹת (נ״ר)
mittens	kfafot	כְּפָפוֹת (נ״ר)
scarf (muffler)	tsa'if	צָעִיף (ז)
glasses (eyeglasses)	miʃka'fayim	מִשְׁקָפַיִים (ז״ר)
umbrella	mitriya	מִטְרִיָּה (נ)

tie (necktie)	aniva	עֲנִיבָה (נ)
handkerchief	mimχata	מִמְחָטָה (נ)
comb	masrek	מַסְרֵק (ז)
hairbrush	miv'reʃet se'ar	מִבְרֶשֶׁת שֵׂיעָר (נ)

buckle	avzam	אַבְזָם (ז)
belt	χagora	חֲגוֹרָה (נ)
purse	tik	תִּיק (ז)

6. House. Apartment

apartment	dira	דִּירָה (נ)
room	'χeder	חֶדֶר (ז)
bedroom	χadar ʃena	חֲדַר שֵׁינָה (ז)
dining room	pinat 'oχel	פִּינַת אוֹכֶל (נ)

living room	salon	סָלוֹן (ז)
study (home office)	χadar avoda	חֲדַר עֲבוֹדָה (ז)
entry room	prozdor	פְּרוֹזְדוֹר (ז)
bathroom (room with a bath or shower)	χadar am'batya	חֲדַר אַמְבַּטְיָה (ז)
half bath	ʃerutim	שֵׁירוּתִים (ז״ר)

vacuum cleaner	ʃo'ev avak	שׁוֹאֵב אָבָק (ז)
mop	magev im smartut	מַגֵּב עִם סְמַרְטוּט (ז)
dust cloth	smartut avak	סְמַרְטוּט אָבָק (ז)
short broom	mat'ate katan	מַטְאֲטֵא קָטָן (ז)
dustpan	ya'e	יָעֶה (ז)

furniture	rehitim	רָהִיטִים (ז״ר)
table	ʃulχan	שׁוּלְחָן (ז)
chair	kise	כִּסֵּא (ז)
armchair	kursa	כּוּרְסָה (נ)

mirror	mar'a	מַרְאָה (נ)
carpet	ʃa'tiaχ	שָׁטִיחַ (ז)
fireplace	aχ	אָח (נ)
drapes	vilonot	וִילוֹנוֹת (ז״ר)
table lamp	menorat ʃulχan	מְנוֹרַת שׁוּלְחָן (נ)
chandelier	niv'reʃet	נִבְרֶשֶׁת (נ)

| kitchen | mitbaχ | מִטְבָּח (ז) |
| gas stove (range) | tanur gaz | תַּנּוּר גָּז (ז) |

electric stove	tanur χaʃmali	תַּנוּר חַשמַלִי (ז)
microwave oven	mikrogal	מִיקרוֹגַל (ז)
refrigerator	mekarer	מְקָרֵר (ז)
freezer	makpi	מַקפִּיא (ז)
dishwasher	me'diaχ kelim	מֵדִיחַ כֵּלִים (ז)
faucet	'berez	בֶּרֶז (ז)
meat grinder	matχenat basar	מַטחֵנַת בָּשָׂר (נ)
juicer	masχeta	מַסחֵטָה (נ)
toaster	'toster	טוֹסטֶר (ז)
mixer	'mikser	מִיקסֶר (ז)
coffee machine	meχonat kafe	מְכוֹנַת קָפֶּה (נ)
kettle	kumkum	קוּמקוּם (ז)
teapot	kumkum	קוּמקוּם (ז)
TV set	tele'vizya	טֶלֶוִויזיָה (נ)
VCR (video recorder)	maχʃir 'vide'o	מַכשִׁיר וִידֵאוֹ (ז)
iron (e.g., steam ~)	maghets	מַגהֵץ (ז)
telephone	'telefon	טֶלֶפוֹן (ז)

Made in the USA
Middletown, DE
27 November 2022

16215922R00051